TEEN SUICIDE & SELF-HARM PREVENTION WORKBOOK

A Clinician's Guide to Assist Teen Clients

Reproducible Activity Handouts and Assessments

Ester R.A. Leutenberg
John J. Liptak, EdD

WholePerson
Associates, Inc.
publisher of therapy, counseling, and self-help resources

WholePerson Associates, Inc.

publisher of therapy, counseling, and self-help resources

Whole Person Associates

101 West 2nd Street, Suite 203
Duluth, MN 55802-5004

800-247-6789

Books@WholePerson.com
WholePerson.com

**Teen Suicide & Self-Harm Prevention Workbook
A Clinican's Guide to Assist Teen Clients**

All efforts have been made to ensure the accuracy of the information
contained in this workbook as of the date published. The authors
and the publisher expressly disclaim responsibility for any adverse
effects arising from the use or application of the information
contained herein.

Editorial Director: Jack Kosmach
Art Director: Mathew Pawlak
Cover Design: Adam Sippola

Library of Congress Control Number: 2019943492
ISBN:978-1-57025-359-1

This workbook is dedicated to
Mitchell A. Leutenberg who died by suicide.
1956 - 1986

His own words give us insight to the daily struggles of mental illness:

One's mental health is more valuable than one's physical well-being and without being at peace little is worth it.
Mitchell A. Leutenberg, 3/17/1985

OUR GOAL FOR THIS WORKBOOK IS TO HELP CLINICIANS GUIDE THEIR CLIENTS IN FINDING PEACE IN LIFE.

Esther Leutenberg   *John J. Liptak*

Our gratitude to all of these professionals who make us look good:

Art Director – Mathew Pawlak
Cover Design – Adam Sippola
Editorial Director – Jack Kosmach
Copy Editor – Peg Johnson
Editor and Life-long Teacher – Eileen Regen
Proof-reader and Reviewer – Jay Leutenberg

Reviewers

Lillie Brittner, TRS, CTRS
Carol Butler Cooper, MS Ed, RN, C
Jackie Daniels Brown, TRS, CTRS
Ruth Coleman, BSW
Annette Damien, MS, PPS
Yetta Dritch
Sue Gallen, RN MS
Sharon Geiger, MA

Mickey Henson, MA
Eileen Jonatis, MA Ed
Sandra Negley, MTRS, CTRS, FDRT
Emily Polichette, MM, SCMT, MT-BC
Melissa Rollins, TRS, CTRS
Vesna Metrovich, Non-Violent Communication Trainer
Niki Tilicki, MA Ed
Dawn Weiss, BS

Our gratitude to the national organizations who allowed us to publish their wise words of wisdom from their websites. See Chapter 6 - Resources.

Teen Suicide & Self-Harm Prevention Workbook

© 2019 WHOLE PERSON ASSOCIATES, 101 WEST 2ND STREET, SUITE 203, DULUTH MN 55802 • 800-247-6789 • WHOLEPERSON.COM

Teen Suicide & Self-Harm Prevention Workbook
A Reproducible Guide for Clinicians to Assist Teen Clients

Free PDF Download Available
To access your free PDF download of the assessment tools
and all of the reproducible activities in this workbook, go to our website:
https://wholeperson.com/store/TeenSuicidePrevention3492.html

Table of Contents

(Continued on the next page)

Teen Suicide & Self-Harm Prevention Workbook
A Reproducible Guide for Clinicians to Assist Teen Clients

Table of Contents *(Continued)*

(Continued on the next page)

Teen Suicide & Self-Harm Prevention Workbook
A Reproducible Guide for Clinicians to Assist Teen Clients

Table of Contents *(Continued)*

Our gratitude to the above organizations
who allowed us to print wise words of
wisdom from their websites!

About Teen Suicide and Self-Harm

Diagnostic and Statistical Manual of Mental Disorders, Volume V (DSM-V)

Suicidal behavior (death and attempts) is usually a complication of psychiatric conditions, most commonly mood disorders. However, it also occurs in schizophrenia, substance use disorders (particularly with alcohol), and personality and anxiety disorders, among others. About 10% of those who commit or attempt suicide have no identifiable psychiatric illness. However, our current nomenclature considers suicidal behavior a symptom of a major depressive episode or borderline personality disorder.

Non-suicidal self-harm (NSSI), defined as the deliberate, self-inflicted destruction of body tissue without suicidal intent and for purposes not socially sanctioned, includes behaviors such as cutting, burning, biting, and scratching skin.

The *Teen Suicide & Self-Harm Prevention Workbook* for teen clients is a proactive approach to dealing with the many characteristics that may prompt teens to experience self-harm and/or suicide ideation. The purpose of this workbook is to provide information and tools that build upon each other to help clients manage thoughts, feelings, and behaviors related to self-harm and suicide.

Definitions Regarding Suicide and Self-Harm

Accidental Death: Any death that occurs as the result of an accident. A death is only deemed accidental if it is not intended (suicide), expected, or foreseeable (illness).

Die by Suicide: This term is now used, as well as *killed himself, or took her own life,* rather than *commit suicide,* which tends to stigmatize suicide. A person who dies by suicide is not committing a sin or crime. Although some religions/cultures may teach otherwise, we (the authors) believe a person who dies by suicide is not committing a sin or crime. A suicide often follows an intolerable trauma or stress, or it is a product of a mental illness. The authors of this workbook prefer the term *die by suicide.*

Dietary Self-Harm: Restricting food for the purpose of self-harm or inducing death; for example, consuming items that will lead to a diabetic event that may lead to an intentional death.

Self-Harm: An intentional, direct harming of an individual's body, self-inflicted without suicidal intent. Other terms such as cutting and self-mutilation are used for self-harm behaviors.

Suicidal Self-Directed Violence: This behavior is self-directed and deliberately results in harm or the potential to harm oneself. There is evidence, whether implicit or explicit, of suicidal intent. This encompasses suicide deaths and suicide attempts.

Suicide Attempt: A suicide attempt occurs when an individual engages in self-directed potentially injurious behavior with the intent to die but the injury does not result in death.

Suicide Ideation: Suicidal ideation occurs when an individual is having thoughts, hearing voices, or preparing plans for a suicide.

Myths about SELF-HARM

It is important to look at self-harm from an objective mindset. Below are some of the myths and misconceptions that surround the topic of self-harm.

MYTH: Only adults self-harm.
People of all ages self-harm. Self-harm is not particularly meant as a suicide attempt. It is an unhealthy attempt to cope with emotional pain such as anger, frustration, loss, sadness, etc., and physical pain.

MYTH: Teens who self-harm are usually open about self-harm behavior.
Self-harm in teens is usually kept private.

MYTH: Teens who self-harm do this as an occasional expression of behavior and only do it once or twice.
Some teens may self-harm once or twice and then stop. However, many teens do it frequently and it becomes a long-term, continual behavior, and possibly a habit.

MYTH: Teens who self-harm use only the cutting behavior.
Teens who self-harm cut or scratch with a sharp object, hit or punch themselves, carve on or pierce the skin, pull out hair, burn, pick at a wound, etc., or continually put themselves in harm's way, i.e., engage in fights, drive recklessly, abuse substances, etc.

MYTH: Only teens with a mental illness consider self-harm.
Not all teens who self-harm have a mental illness, but they may have emotional, physical, and/or social issues that create unbearable emotions that lead to extreme physical responses.

MYTH: Teens who self-harm are willing to talk about it with others.
Usually, teens who self-harm do not share with other teens. It is vital for the person having self-harm thoughts or behaviors to talk with someone they trust: a therapist, friend, family member, spiritual or religious leader, etc.

MYTH: Self-harm calms the person for a long time.
In fact, the person usually feels guilt, shame, and other painful emotions afterwards.

MYTH: No real damage happens with self-harm.
There is a strong possibility that serious or life-threatening consequences can occur from self-injuring behaviors.

MYTH: Teens self-harm for attention.
Teens who self-harm should not be considered attention-seeking. Teens self-harm for many reasons: to help themselves feel something when they are emotionally numb; to distract themselves from their emotional pain; to punish themselves; or to disfigure themselves.

Although these are only a few of the myths and misconceptions about self-harm, they will provide you with some insight into the thinking that is prevalent about people who self-harm. Encourage individuals to call a trusted person, see a mental health facilitator or medical professional, find a positive support system, and use local or national resources and hotlines.

Myths about SUICIDE

It is important to look at suicide from an objective mindset. Below are some of the myths and misconceptions that surround the topic of suicide.

MYTH: Most teens die by suicide without any warning.
Many suicidal teens have long histories of mental health issues, trauma, and maladaptive behavior. In addition, most teens who die by suicide exhibit warning signs such as making a will, giving away belongings, reckless behavior, and/or self-isolation.

MYTH: Teens who talk about suicide are trying to get attention and won't really do it.
Most suicidal teens do not seek attention, they seek empathy. They want understanding and want people to know how they feel.

MYTH: Once someone has already decided to die by suicide, no one person or thing is going to stop them. They just want to die.
Most suicidal teens are often ambivalent about their decision and are torn between wanting to die and wanting to live. Most suicidal individuals don't want death but want their pain to stop. With an effective support system and the use of preventative tools and techniques, they can receive and benefit from help.

MYTH: After a person has attempted suicide, it is unlikely the person will try again.
Teens who have attempted suicide are very likely to try again. They need professional help and a reliable support system that is alert to the warning signs of suicidal crisis.

MYTH: Only teens with a mental illness consider suicide.
Not all teens who die by suicide have mental health problems at the time of their death; however, many do.

MYTH: If teens survive a suicide attempt, then they were not serious about ending their life.
All attempts, including self-harm, should be taken as a serious attempt to end one's life.

MYTH: Discussing suicide with someone may cause that teen to consider it or make things worse.
Talking about suicide with a trusted person can be one of the most effective means of helping teens. Asking teens if they're suicidal will not give them the idea to die by suicide if they haven't thought about it already. Many suicidal teens are truthful and relieved when asked about their feelings and intentions. This can be the first step in helping suicidal teens make the choice to live.

> Although the above are only a few myths and misconceptions about suicide, they provide insight into the irrational thinking prevalent in society. These myths and misconceptions interfere with a suicidal person's attempt to get help, enhance overall well-being, and develop a positive outlook in life. Encourage and guide individuals to call a trusted person, see a mental health facilitator or medical professional, find a positive support system, and use local or national resources and hotlines.

Ways Teens Self-Harm

A teen may...

- Abuse substances.
- Bang on or punch objects to the point of bruising or bleeding.
- Become anorexic or bulimic.
- Bite oneself to the point that bleeding occurs or marks remain on the skin.
- Break one's own bones.
- Burn wrists, hands, arms, legs, torso, or other areas of the body.
- Carve words or symbols into skin.
- Cut wrists, arms, legs, or other areas of the body.
- Deprive oneself of sleep.
- Drip acid onto skin.
- Engage in reckless behavior in hope of self-harm.
- Exercise excessively in an unhealthy way.
- Ingest a caustic substance.
- Ingest a sharp object.
- Pick a fight with the intention of getting hurt.
- Prevent wounds from healing.
- Punch oneself to the point of bruising or bleeding.
- Rip or tear skin.
- Scratch or pinch with fingernails or other objects to the point that bleeding occurs or marks remain on the skin.
- Stick sharp objects such as glass, needles, pins, and staples into or underneath the skin.
- Take part in aggressive activities with the intention of getting hurt.

Suicide Risk Factors

A number of personal, individual, biological, social, relational, and environmental factors contribute to the risk of self-harm or suicide attempts. These factors may not cause a person to have thoughts of self-harm or suicide, but combined they may increase the risk for some individuals:

- Access to lethal tools
- Bullying others – in person or online
- Bullying victim – in person or online
- Celebrities or heroes who die by suicide
- Changing, misusing, or stopping meds
- Childhood trauma and abuse
- Family history of suicide
- History of alcohol and/or substance abuse
- History of depression
- Inability to find and connect with supportive people
- Past and/or present mental health issues
- Refusal to seek help (often due to stigma)
- Lack of problem-solving skills
- Lack of support
- Non-acceptance by family, community, and/or society
- Movies or television shows that glorify suicide
- People they know who self-injure
- Physical illness and chronic pain
- Previous suicide attempts
- Significant losses (relationships, pets, work, death of family and friends, financial, etc.)
- Social isolation

> Research suggests that the presence of one of the above factors,
> or a combination of several or many of these factors, may put a person at risk.
> The more factors a person is experiencing, the more that person may be at risk.

Protective Factors

Many protective factors exist to buffer people from self-harm, suicidal ideation, and/or attempting suicide:

- Access to a variety of healthcare services
- Assistance in monitoring thoughts and processing feelings
- Consistent support from friends and family
- Effective treatment for psychological issues, physical health problems, and substance abuse problems
- Engaging in productive activities can decrease risk factors
- Ongoing support from healthcare services
- Stress management, coping, decision making, problem solving, and mindfulness skills

> It is important to utilize as many of these protective factors as possible.
> The more factors that are accessible,
> the greater the chances for those in need to redirect their lives.

Information for the Clinician about the Suicide and Self-Harm Prevention Workbook
A Reproducible Guide for Clinicians to Assist Teen Clients
By John J. Liptak, EdD and Ester R.A. Leutenberg

Before using this workbook with clients,
please read all of the points below and on the next page.

1. The *Suicide and Self-Harm Prevention Workbook* is designed to be used with clients in the care of a trained clinician.

2. This workbook is a practical, step-by-step guide to present a detailed understanding of the context in which self-harm and suicide play out in a person's life, warning signs and risk factors experienced by teens suffering with thoughts and actions of hurting themselves, ways to prevent suicide ideation, and methods for finding a healthy support network.

3. Clinicians are responsible for ensuring the health, well-being, and safety of the person or teens with whom they work while using this workbook. Clinicians will need to use their clinical judgment while utilizing the materials contained in this workbook. Clinical judgment includes deciding how each of the handouts and activities can best be used to help their clients achieve maximum health and wellness, while working to resolve feelings, thoughts, and behaviors related to self-harm and suicidal ideation.

4. Our goal for this workbook is not to diagnose a client's potential for self-harm or suicidal ideation, or even for the clinician to make a mental health diagnosis from this workbook's content. Our goal is to touch on some of the symptoms and possibilities, create realizations, and provide coping methods which will help teens to go forward and consider the possibility of a need for further medical help, medications, and therapy. Mental health issues of any kind are not to be stigmatized, nor should anyone need to feel like a victim of stereotyping.

Most importantly, our goal for this workbook is to help clients recognize that many other people have many of the same issues, no shame is to be connected, self-harm and/or suicide is definitely not the answer to their problems.

(Continued on the next page)

Information for the Clinician
about this Workbook *(Continued)*

5. The pages of this workbook can be used in a variety of ways:

*   Activities can be used with individual clients alone, in pairs, or in a very small group. If there is more than one person, the activities can be completed individually and then shared with each other, as long as all of the participants are comfortable doing so.

*   Individual clients or small group members can complete the activities with the help of a clinician, if needed. When utilizing this approach, clinicians will also help their clients process their responses to the various activities they have completed.

*   Small group members can utilize the activities as part of the therapeutic process. When using this approach, they can process the information together with other group members to help achieve commonality and optimal results.

*   If there is more than one client, explain that this will be a *"What is said in this room, stays in this room"* session. Explain to the clients that to insure privacy, they need to use a name code when writing about or talking about other people in their lives. *(Ex: H.H.M. might be, **He helps me!**)* Don't use a person's initials.

*   If there is a very small group, it is often successful to have group members work together in pairs. When utilizing this approach, be sure to pair group members based on willingness to work together. Pairs can process information together, role play, or work as a team in a group discussion.

*   All of the materials contained in the chapters of this workbook can be utilized in an individual or a very small group setting. If the clinician is using this workbook with a small group, you may photocopy or print enough materials for the members in the group, or allow individuals to reflect, write, and then process the materials together. The clinician can pick and choose the reflection activities that will best assist clients to overcome their desire to self-injure or die by suicide.

> If at any time, while using these materials, you fear that a client is not progressing, or that a client's condition is worsening, seek or recommend the assistance of a medical/mental health professional as soon as possible.

Layout of the Workbook

This workbook consists of reproducible materials for use by mental health professionals and health care providers in their work with an individual teen and/or with very small groups.

It is usually difficult for troubled people to express their feelings or their thoughts. The purpose of these activity handouts is for participants to build confidence to open up by completing interesting and appealing pages, and writing words that are challenging to think about or say.

- The first page of each chapter introduces the chapter topic to the facilitator and the fourth page introduces the topic to the participants.
- The second and third pages are treatment planning options for clinicians working with individuals or small groups.

Activity Handouts

Activity handouts ask participants for opinions and facts about their feelings and beliefs. The accuracy and usefulness of the information is dependent on the information that clients honestly provide about themselves. Assure clients that they do not need to share their information if they do not want to do so, nor do they need to show the handout to anyone but the clinician. Assure them that they are in a safe place and they can be honest.

Activity Handouts...

- Help clinicians quickly and easily learn details about each client's life to enhance the treatment process.
- Assist clients in the reflection process so that they gain insight and engage in behavioral change.
- Help clinicians in the exploration of progress made by clients as they continue to develop skills and integrate them into their daily lives.
- Help clients learn more about how their thinking, management of feelings, and behaviors are affecting their thoughts of self-harm and suicide.
- Provide clinicians with a process for initiating discussions about sensitive topics like self-harm and suicide ideation.
- Provide clients with ways to tell their stories as they work collaboratively with clinicians.
- Serve as a great aid in developing plans for effective change and positive outlook in life, both in the present and in the future.
- Allow clients to explore various elements of themselves and their situations.
- Encourage clients to not pigeonhole or stereotype people.
- Serve as exploratory exercises and not a judgment of who they are as human beings.

These exercises and activities should never be considered a substitute for professional assistance.
If you feel any of your participants need more assistance than you can provide, or another person to also assist them as well as yourself, refer them to an appropriate professional.

(Continued on the next page)

Activity Handouts (*Continued*)

Not every handout needs to be used, or used in the order of this workbook's presentation. The clinician can pick and choose chapters and activity handouts as needed.

The activity handouts are reflective, easy-to-use exercises, presented in a variety of formats to accommodate multiple intelligences and different learning styles. Their purpose is to help clients examine their past, learn coping and problem-solving skills in the present, and plan for a hope-filled future. Many of the activities allow clients to utilize the power of journaling about important topics related to their current situation. These activities will serve as a base for the facilitator to gently delve into the contents of each participant's responses.

Self-exploration activities assist clients in self-reflection, enhance self-knowledge, identify potential ineffective behaviors, and teach more effective ways of coping with the thoughts and stressors in their lives. They are designed to help teens make a series of discoveries that lead to enhanced life skills, as well as to serve as an energizing way to help reduce thoughts of self-harm and suicide. These brief, easy-to-use self-reflection tools are designed to promote insight and self-growth. Many different types of guided self-exploration activities are provided for you to pick and choose the activities that are most needed by your clients and the ones that will be most appealing to them. The unique features of the exploration activities make them user-friendly and appropriate for a variety of individual sessions and very small group sessions.

All of the activities are reproducible and can be tailored to the specific needs of the individual client or a very small group. In some activities, participants will have an opportunity to:

- Explore how they could make changes in their lives to feel better. These activities are designed to help participants reflect on their current life situations, discover new ways of living more peacefully, and implement changes in their lives to accommodate these skills.
- Journal as a way of enhancing their self-awareness. Using journaling prompts, participants will be able to write about the thoughts, attitudes, feelings, and behaviors that have contributed to, or are currently contributing to, their current situation. Through journaling, participants are able to safely address their concerns.
- Examine mood issues by delving into past behaviors for negative patterns and learning new ways of facing issues more effectively in the future. These activities are designed to help participants reflect on their lives in ways that will allow them to develop healthier lifestyles.

Each clinician has the choice of how and with whom to process the activities:
With individuals, a very small group, pairs, volunteers sharing, etc.

Activity Handouts Come in Many Forms!

- Assessments
- Check-off Lists
- Descriptions
- Drawing
- Journaling Reflections

- Quotations
- Reminders
- Responses
- Self-Exploration

 © 2019 WHOLE PERSON ASSOCIATES, 101 WEST 2ND STREET, SUITE 203, DULUTH MN 55802 • 800-247-6789 • WHOLEPERSON.COM

Assessments

Each chapter's first activity handout is an assessment:
Self-Harm - Self-Harm Behavior Evaluation
Warning Signs - Suicide Warning Signs Check-Up
Risk Factors - Risk Factors Insights
Prevention - A Self-Reflection Survey
Support - A Support System Review

These assessments can be used by clinicians to quickly and easily gather self-reported data from their client(s). They are not designed to be diagnostic like many traditional assessments. Their purpose is to gather information from the clients quickly to better understand them. Each of the assessments is set up so that they can be completed collaboratively between clients and clinicians. Clients may be able to assess themselves before turning the handout over to the clinician, however, the clinician is responsible for interpreting the information derived from the assessments for and with the client. The intent is not to pigeonhole clients based on the results.

The assessments in each of the chapters are helpful in many different ways:

- Establish a behavioral baseline from which facilitators and participants can gauge progress toward identified goals.

- Help clinicians gather valuable information about their clients.

- Help clinicians in the measurement of progress over the process of treatment.

- Serve as pre-tests and post-tests to measure changes in thoughts, feelings, and behaviors related to self-harm and suicidal ideation.

- Help clinicians to identify patterns that are positively and negatively affecting their clients.

- Provide and prompt insight and positive behavioral change in clients.

- Help clients feel part of the treatment-planning process as they work collaboratively with clinicians.

- Provide clinicians with a starting point to begin to learn more about their clients' strengths and limitations.

When working with small groups, the clinician will observe how each client might react differently to the results and how clients differ in the ways that they process the results and integrate them into their thinking.

The accuracy and usefulness of the information is dependent on the information that clients honestly provide about themselves. Assure clients that they do not need to share their information if they do not want to do so. Most importantly, they need to feel safe and be honest.

These assessments should never be considered a substitute for professional assistance. If you feel any of your clients need more assistance than you can provide, refer them to an appropriate professional.

Providing Feedback

Reassure clients that the completed handouts will be seen only by you, the clinician, as well as anyone else with whom the participant decides to share the results. Encourage clients to be honest!

When providing feedback, attempt to set the client at ease by discussing how you will provide feedback about their writings. You might want to ask if there is anything they want to offer or clarify about the handout before they begin work. Remind clients to complete each handout to the best of their ability and then return it to you.

When preparing to provide feedback, explain that the data obtained from the completed handout is a way for you and the clients to gain insight into their unique view of the world. These activities can help them make sense of what is happening in their lives, how they express their own ideas, and how they see themselves in the world.

Discussing the Handout

Some ways to get the most out of a feedback session:

- Ask the clients if they have any questions about the handout.
- Ask the clients if they were honest.
- Discuss the handout as soon as possible. Clients might worry about the things they wrote.
- Begin feedback sessions with something positive. People can hear limitations better if they have first heard about their strengths.
- You might want to begin with a simple thought or question and move to the more complex ones. Too much information all at once may be overwhelming.
- Begin with findings the clients will accept. Gradually move on to something they may have considered, but have not recognized fully or reflected on.
- Be gentle. Some clients may become defensive when hearing feedback about their responses.
- Choose your language very carefully. Be as positive and as optimistic as you possibly can be.
- End feedback sessions with a positive note. This may help offset any negative feedback you gave that was more difficult to hear. It can also allow clients to feel that even though they have issues, things are not all bad.
- Some other things to remember:
  - Avoid complex jargon.
  - Use clear, simple language the clients can understand.
  - Use positive, action-oriented language.
  - Personalize when possible.
  - Ask the client to tell a narrative or story about the results.
  - Avoid information overload.

After Feedback Sessions

As you near the end of a feedback session, wrap up by providing an overview of what you gleaned from the results and how the results can help you and the clients to develop a plan for treatment and a goal-setting tool.

Considerations for this phase:

- Enlist the clients in verifying or modifying activity findings. If they disagree, ask if they can understand how others might perceive them this way. Ask if they can think of any situations in which the feedback might be true. If they believe these things may be true for other people but not for them, ask if they can think of any characteristics they might have in common with the people for whom these statements would be true.

- Pause and support the clients' affective reactions as they occur. The feedback you have given them may be hard to understand or accept. Even if they knew it and understood it, it may be very hard to hear it stated clearly, or very hard to accept these aspects of themselves.

- Never argue with a client about a list or evaluation finding. Some of it may be very true and some less true for the client. Some may be true in most settings and some only in a few.

- The point of the feedback session is to gain understanding and clarity of the life issues of each client. On the other hand, the final meaning of the results is the interpretation you give to the data, as it is your professional opinion.

- A common reaction to receiving feedback is a feeling of defensiveness. When this occurs:
  - Talk privately with those who may feel threatened.
  - Balance negatives with many positives.
  - Be gentle and sensitive in your approach.
  - Provide corroborating information.
  - Acknowledge possible limitations in your assessment methods.
  - Help clients identify possible solutions and set goals for greater well-being.

Moving from Activity Results to Action

After an activity has been completed, you can move on to the next step in the process. This step involves clients reflecting on their life and taking action to improve it.

- One way is that clinicians focus on the areas in which clients show the greatest weaknesses, and thus have the most prominent issues to be resolved.
- Another way is exploring the client's major strengths to build positivity.

The way that you utilize the activities in the workbook will be based on your beliefs about the best way to approach the treatment process.

Other Features of this Workbook

Quotations
At the end of each chapter, there is a page with one or two quotations relating to the chapter, for the participants' reflection and journaling activities. These quotations are effective in helping clients to apply their thoughts about the quotations to their own life. Reading metaphors for their own life, clients can see the wisdom behind the words of others, reflect on how each quote is related to the life they are living, and apply the wisdom when appropriate. Quotes can be motivational and prompt clients to take positive action.

Practical Resources
At the end of this workbook, participants will be exposed to a variety of resources that they can access when they are stressed. These resources can be used by clients and clinicians to learn more about self-harm and suicide prevention, hotline information, organizations that are available to provide help, etc. The materials can be photocopied and distributed to clients and their family members as needed.

Reproducibility
The activities in this workbook are reproducible. This means you can give each participant a page to talk about, complete with the clinician, take home as a reminder, or to complete independently at home. You may give them extra pages for independent reflection as well.

Confidentiality Using Name Codes

Before you begin to use the materials in this workbook explain to clients that confidentiality is a term for any action that preserves the privacy of other people with whom they have interacted in the past or with whom they are currently interacting.

Instruct the participants to use NAME CODES when writing or speaking about anyone in their past, current, or future lives. This is an important aspect of confidentiality when talking about sensitive subjects like self-harm and suicide.

Clients completing the activities in this workbook might be asked to respond to events that are currently occurring or have happened in the past, and to write about others in their lives. Name codes are especially important when working with a pair or a group. Confidentiality shows respect for others and allows – even encourages – people to explore their feelings without hurting anyone's feelings or fearing gossip, harm, or retribution.

Examples of Name Codes:
   J.L.A. might mean a friend named Jane who Loves Animals
   L.P.P. might mean Loves Pepperoni Pizza
   V.L.H. might mean Volunteers at the Local Hospital

Chapter Descriptions

*Each chapter begins with a table of contents and
treatment planning options for clinicians of individuals and small groups
to engage in prior to distributing the actual activity.*

Self-Harm
This chapter will help clinicians to assist clients identify and explore their self-harm actions as well as discover and implement some tools, skills, and techniques for overcoming this behavior.

Warning Signs
This chapter will assist clinicians to help clients recognize, identify, and explore the warning signs and the effects that these signs have on their self-harm or suicidal thoughts.

Risk Factors
This chapter will assist clinicians to help clients explore their various risk factors and ways they can reduce the effects of these risk factors when experiencing a crisis.

Prevention
This chapter will assist clinicians to provide clients with tools, skills, and techniques for receiving help and reducing their self-harming and suicidal ideation.

Support
This chapter will assist clinicians to provide clients with ways to access a variety of needed support people as well as community resources.

Client and Clinician National Resources
This chapter will provide clients and clinicians information about self-harm and suicide prevention from national resources.

Free PDF Download Available
To access your free PDF download of the assessment tools
and all of the reproducible activities in this workbook, go to our website:
https://wholeperson.com/store/TeenSuicidePrevention3492.html

CHAPTER 1

Self-Harm

INTRODUCTION FOR THE CLINICIAN

Self-harm is any behavior which involves the deliberate causing of pain to oneself.

Although self-harm is not the same as attempting to die by suicide, it can be a predictor of a future suicide. Self-harm is usually a sign of emotional distress, trauma, neglect, abuse, etc. It is not an indicator of a mental illness, or reserved for those who have a mental illness. It is a behavior of those who need to learn coping skills in order to identify and manage their underlying emotions.

Teens who harm themselves tend to feel empty inside, and they experience over or understimulation. They are often unable to express their feelings, may feel lonely, believe they are not understood by others, and can be fearful of various relationships and responsibilities. Self-harm is a way of trying to cope with or relieve painful and hard-to-express feelings. The problem is that the relief experienced is temporary, and without proper treatment a self-destructive cycle often develops. Self-harm can also be a way to try to gain control over one's body when nothing else can be controlled in life.

By engaging in self-harm behaviors, teens attempt to gain relief from a negative feeling or mental state, resolve an interpersonal issue, deal with feelings of boredom and/or create more positive feelings.

This chapter will help you to help your clients take these actions:

- Assess and explore their self-harming behavior.
- Discover how thoughts, feelings, and actions are intertwined.
- Reflect and identify specific triggers to self-harming.

Self-Harm

Treatment Planning Options for Clinicians Working with Individuals and Small Groups.

Each item is related to an assessment or activity page in the workbook and presents additional ideas for adapting each exercise when working with individuals and/or small groups. They can be used at the discretion of the clinician prior to using the activity. Each idea can also be used to help participants process their learning related to the material covered on each page after using the handout.

28	**Self-Harm Behavior Evaluation**
Individuals	Respond to a list of the reasons the person may deliberately cause pain or harm to him or herself.
Small Group	Discuss the concept that secrets can kill and disclosure can elicit empathy, hope, a better life, etc.
29	**Process for the Self-Harm Behavior Evaluation Scores**
Individuals	Together with the clinician, explore the list of responses checked off on the Behavior Evaluation.
Small Group	Together with the clinician and others, explore the responses checked off on the Behavior Evaluation.
31	**Describe Emotional Pain**
Individuals	Identify features of their emotional pain by completing sentence-starter text boxes.
Small Group	Clinician cuts out the text boxes; each person picks up a cutout and responds aloud.
32	**Environmental Self-Exploration**
Individuals	Identify the people, places, methods and possible patterns of their self-harm.
Small Group	Participants take turns as moderators and ask the questions of peer panelists.
33	**Keeping Busy**
Individuals	Identify positive people, projects, and activities to engage in to diminish self-harm.
Small Group	The group discusses and lists their ideas.
34	**Gentle Reminders**
Individuals	Note positive self-talk, action alternatives, support persons, and post-it messages.
Small Group	Clinician cuts out the boxes and gives one to each person to complete. Participants share results.
35	**My Self-Harm Triggers**
Individuals	Respond to specific emotions, note their triggers and more effective ways to cope.
Small Group	Clinician lists emotions on the board; participants choose one and share their triggers.
36	**Time to Change Your Routine**
Individuals	Show specific steps in their self-harm routines; read about changing these.
Small Group	Volunteers show their steps on the board; peers state ways to change each step and stop the process.

(Continued on the next page)

Self-Harm *(Continued)*

Treatment Planning Options for Clinicians Working with Individuals and Small Groups.

37	**Thoughts, Emotions, and Behaviors**
Individuals	Depict or describe a situation and the thoughts and feelings that preceded a self-harm behavior.
Small Group	Share their responses and receive peer suggestions about more positive ways to view the situation.
38	**Change Your Thinking**
Individuals	Practice thought changing techniques: Challenge, Stop!, Reframe, and Replace.
Small Group	Share a negative thought; peers give examples of ways to Challenge, Stop!, Reframe, and Replace the thought.
39	**Alternatives to Self-Harm**
Individuals	Respond to a list of alternatives to self-harm participant is willing to try.
Small Group	Discuss the possible pros and cons of each listed alternative.
40	**The 4 D's**
Individuals	Give an example of each technique to prevent self-harm: Delay, Distract, Divert, Defuse.
Small Group	Facilitator lists the 4 D's on the board; participants discuss ways to implement each.
41	**How About Being Kind to Yourself?**
Individuals	Respond to items indicating ways to be to be kind to oneself that the participant is willing to try.
Small Group	Members share their three "most likely to try" and "least likely to try" techniques and explain why.
42	**Let's Have Fun with Healthy and Unhealthy Self-Talk**
Individuals	Draw oneself and create word bubbles showing healthy and unhealthy self-talk text.
Small Group	Suggest a list of positive self-talk messages. Photograph, photocopy or electronically distribute.
43	**Quotes about Self-Harm**
Individuals	Journal about ways to apply the three therapeutic quotations to one's life.
Small Group	Share a quote of their own pertaining to self-harm that they would like to pass on to others.

Self-Harm

INTRODUCTION FOR THE PARTICIPANT

Self-harm is any behavior which involves the deliberate causing of pain to oneself.

Although it is not the same as attempting to die by suicide, it can be a predictor of a future suicide.

It is usually a sign of emotional distress, trauma, neglect, abuse, etc.

Self-harm is not an indicator of a mental illness, or reserved for those who have a mental illness.

It is a behavior of people who need to learn coping skills in order to identify and manage their underlying emotions.

Self-Harm Behavior Evaluation
Introduction and Directions

Self-Harm is often used as a way of coping with negative events and feelings. Teens who self-harm need to understand and identify their destructive thoughts, feelings, and actions.

It is important to explore the reasons why you might be trying to harm yourself.

- This evaluation contains 35 reasons that people harm themselves.
- Read each of the statements and decide whether it describes you or not.
- If the statement does describe you, place a check in the box.
- If the statement does not describe you, leave the box blank.
- If some of your reasons are not listed, write them in the "Other" lines at the bottom.

EXAMPLE:

(This statement describes you.)

☑ To alleviate my pain

(This statement does not describe you.)

☐ To alleviate my pain

This is not a test.
Since there are no right or wrong answers, don't spend too much time thinking about them. Your first reaction is usually the most accurate. Be sure to read them and check those that describe you.

(Turn to the next page and begin.)

Self-Harm Behavior Survey

Check off the boxes to indicate the reasons you deliberately cause pain or harm to yourself.

- ☐ To alleviate my pain.
- ☐ To atone for my mistakes.
- ☐ To avoid dying by suicide.
- ☐ To be noticed.
- ☐ To change my emotional pain into physical pain.
- ☐ To cope with my feelings.
- ☐ To deal with boredom.
- ☐ To do what a friend did to feel better.
- ☐ To encourage or cause others to pay attention to me.
- ☐ To express my feelings physically.
- ☐ To feel relief from a negative situation.
- ☐ To follow through on my urges.
- ☐ To forget.
- ☐ To gain control of my body.
- ☐ To get rid of my feelings of worthlessness.
- ☐ To ignore my problem.
- ☐ To let go of the numbness inside of me.
- ☐ To listen to my inner voice.
- ☐ To live a life of happiness, not depression.
- ☐ To make sure I don't hurt myself in bigger ways.
- ☐ To manage my frustration.
- ☐ To overcome my sadness.
- ☐ To punish myself.
- ☐ To quiet my thoughts of shame.
- ☐ To rejuvenate my energy.
- ☐ To release tension.
- ☐ To relieve my stress.
- ☐ To resolve a disagreement.
- ☐ To rid myself of the emptiness I feel.
- ☐ To shift the attention.
- ☐ To shock people.
- ☐ To show how much I hate myself.
- ☐ To squelch my anger.
- ☐ To stop dwelling on my terrible thoughts.
- ☐ To worry other people.
- ☐ Other _____
- ☐ Other _____
- ☐ Other _____

Discuss this survey with your clinician.

Process for the Self-Harm Behavior Evaluation

The *Self-Harm Behavior Survey* that your client just completed is designed to measure some of the reasons this person might be self-injuring. This *Self-Harm Behavior Evaluation* is intended to help participants begin to think about 35 of the primary reasons cited for self-injurious behavior. Self-evaluations are used for a variety of reasons including:

- An evaluation form is designed to be less threatening than traditional assessments and quizzes, yet provide valuable information about self-injurious behavior for both the participant and the facilitator. You should explain that there are no correct or incorrect answers and that the reasons the participant lists can be helpful in exploring issues related to self-harming behavior.

- Having participants talk about and write about the circumstance related to their self-harming behavior can be therapeutic in and of itself. By writing, participants can move past negative emotions like guilt and shame, access positive emotions like optimism and empathy, and feel connected to others with similar issues. Writing has been shown to enhance personal growth, increase emotional expression, and help a person feel a sense of empowerment and control over life. Remember to ask participants to just sit and write, and not be concerned with grammar or punctuation.

- Self-evaluations encourage participants to become active contributors in the counseling process. Rather than being a simple passive recipient of feedback from the facilitator, participants are empowered, given a voice, and can inform the direction that the counseling process takes. Participants tend to be more engaged in setting goals and working toward these goals when they are active participants in the process.

- Evaluations provide insight into each participant's behavior as well as their perceptions about specific situations. Differences in how you perceive participants and how they perceive themselves will be evident during the completion of this activity. You can use these differences in perceptions throughout the counseling process.

- It's human nature to want to feel that we've been heard. An evaluation gives a voice to people who want to be heard and understood. Allow participants as much time as they need to process the information related to self-harming behaviors. It is important and will provide you with many cues about each participant and his or her issues.

Help the client make a list of the responses checked off on the Self-Harm Behavior Survey. On the following page on the lines under each response, you or your client can write about the reason and then explain the circumstances that create this apparent need.

Self-Harm Behavior Evaluation

The *Self-Harm Behavior Evaluation* that your client just completed is designed to measure some of the reasons this person might be self-harming.

Help the client make a list of the responses checked off on the *Self-Harm Behavior Evaluation.* On the lines under each response, you or your client can write about the reason and then explain the circumstances that create this apparent need. If there are more than six, use another piece of paper

1) I checked off_____

The circumstances:_____

_____

_____

2) I checked off_____

The circumstances:_____

_____

_____

3) I checked off_____

The circumstances:_____

_____

_____

4) I checked off_____

The circumstances:_____

_____

_____

5) I checked off_____

The circumstances:_____

_____

_____

6) I checked off_____

The circumstances:_____

_____

_____

Who is another person (or people) in your life with whom you can share this page?

_____

_____

© 2019 WHOLE PERSON ASSOCIATES, 101 WEST 2ND STREET, SUITE 203, DULUTH MN 55802 • 800-247-6789 • WHOLEPERSON.COM

Describe Emotional Pain

Many teens harm themselves in an attempt to deal with their emotional pain. Self-harm is often an attempt to create a physical feeling of pain to mask the emotional feelings or pain.

Think about your emotional pain. Even though it may be difficult, try to describe it.

My emotional pain feels like ...

My emotional pain causes me to ...

My emotional pain reminds me of ...

My emotional pain is so strong, that I ...

My emotional pain looks like ...

Environmental Self-Exploration

Thinking about the environment in which you harm yourself can provide insight that can help you limit your harmful behavior. Changing the environment can be done when the urge to self-harm strikes. Changing your environment is definitely easier to do before the urge to self-harm occurs.

The first step is figuring out what role the environment plays on your self-harm behavior.

Note the last time you self-harmed._____

Who were you with last? *(Use name codes)*   Are you usually with this person before you self-harm? Why or why not?
Where were you?   Are you usually in this place when you self-harm? Why or why not?
What time of the day or night did this occur?   Is it usually at this time when you self-harm? Why or why not?
How did you self-injure yourself?   Is this your usual method of self-harm? Why or why not?
What prompted your self-harming behavior.   Is this usually what prompts your self-harming behavior? Why or why not?

Looking at your responses above, which patterns or routines are constant? Explain._____

_____

_____

_____

What do you think is a healthy way to replace these patterns or routines?_____

_____

_____

_____

Keeping Busy

Sitting around and thinking about your problems, difficulties, aggravations, runaway emotions, etc., can be detrimental. It allows unwanted, often negative, thoughts to circulate through your head. One way to stop this from happening is to keep yourself busy with positive people, projects, volunteer job or work, hobbies, entertainment, etc.

If you can keep yourself busy and calm at the times of day you are likely to self-harm, you may be able to break that time-related self-harm pattern.

Journal about some ways you can keep busy during the times when you are most at-risk.

Time(s) I am most likely to self-harm: _____

Ways I Can Keep Busy	How I Can do This	Why I Chose This Way
Example: Listen to music.	*In a room alone, with music on my phone.*	*I love music; it is very calming to me!*

Gentle Reminders

Often self-harm becomes a routine of which you may not be consciously aware. When this happens, it is helpful to give yourself gentle reminders to break the routine. When you are faced with the urge to self-harm because you are anxious or having a panic attack, begin by reminding yourself of all the choices that you have.

Journal about how you can provide yourself with the gentle reminders below.

Tell myself that I do not want to physically harm myself anymore. I can say this to myself: _____ _____ _____ _____ _____ _____	**Get help so that I do not cause harm to my body anymore.** I can reach out and contact someone I trust: _____ _____ _____ _____ _____ _____
Tell myself that I do not need to injure myself just because I'm thinking about self-harm. I can do something positive: _____ _____ _____ _____ _____	**Write notes to myself:** "I do not deserve to be harmed." I can post these notes in these places: _____ _____ _____ _____ _____

You always have the choice to __NOT__ harm yourself.
It is up to you to decide if you have control of your body!

My Self-Harm Triggers

One of the steps to recovery from self-harm is the identification and understanding of what triggers you to harm yourself. By recognizing these triggers, you can determine the function your self-harming behavior serves; you can learn other ways to get those needs met and thus reduce the need to hurt yourself. Self-harm is most often a way of dealing with emotional pain.

The first step in understanding your triggers is to identify the feelings that make you want to self-harm. Below, list why you feel these emotions, and how you can better manage them. Use Name Codes.

My Emotions	What Causes These Feelings	How I Can Deal With Them More Effectively
Example: Lonely	*Death of my pet*	*Visit other pets at the animal shelter*
Angry		
Anxious or Stressed		
Ashamed or Embarrassed		
Empty or Void of Feelings		
Fearful		
Frustrated		
Guilt		
Helpless or Hopeless		
Lonely		
Sad		
Other		

Discuss responses in the last column with your clinician.

Time to Change Your Routine

Most teens who harm themselves do so by following a specific routine that includes time, place, and action. It is important to identify your specific routines in order to stop yourself from self-harm. Changing your routines will probably make you uncomfortable. This discomfort can help you to realize what is happening and help you to stop your self-harm.

List every single little action of your routines of self-harm.
(Example: I check to see if anyone is home, I turn off my cell phone,
I turn the lights off, etc. Afterwards I …)

My Self-Harm Routines

Thoughts, Emotions, and Behaviors

One tool to help you understand your self-harm triggers and your thought patterns that often prompt these triggers, is to keep a Thoughts, Emotions, and Behavior Journal. Because thoughts often precede emotions which precede behaviors *(I think it is my fault ... then I feel guilty ... then I self-injure)*, it is important to journal your thoughts.

Writing down these feelings or drawing a picture of the experience will help identify patterns that lead to self-harm and provide an outlet to express your feelings and process your thoughts.

When you feel the urge to self-harm, or when you actually do harm yourself, write or draw the situation, thoughts, and feelings that preceded your experience.

The goal is to become more aware of your thoughts and how they lead to negative emotions and behaviors.

A Time I Felt the Urge and Self-Harmed.

Change Your Thinking

Your negative, and possibly unreal thinking, can be at the heart of self-harming behavior. There are many different ways to alter your thinking when you begin to feel negative emotions and think about harming yourself. Try all of these and then pick and choose those that work most effectively for you.

Write about how you can try all of these different techniques to change your thinking.
Use Name Codes.

Challenge: You can challenge the negative thoughts. *(Example: "It was all my fault!")* You will learn that many of these thoughts are not true, but only feel true at the time. *(Example: "It may not have been my fault. Maybe it was something I could not control.")*

_____

_____

_____

Stop: If you find yourself in a spiral of negative thoughts, think (or even shout) the word **"STOP!"** and change your thoughts to something else.

_____

_____

_____

Reframe: You can reframe negative thoughts. To do this, assign a new meaning based on your interpretation of the situation. *(Example: Thinking "I should have been there more for her." could be reframed as "I had to take care of my family also. I was there for her as much as I possibly could have been.")*

_____

_____

_____

Replace: You can replace negative thoughts with positive ones.
(Example: "I am a terrible person." can be replaced with "I am a good person who did the best I could at that particular moment in time.")

_____

_____

_____

© 2019 WHOLE PERSON ASSOCIATES, 101 WEST 2ND STREET, SUITE 203, DULUTH MN 55802 • 800-247-6789 • WHOLEPERSON.COM

Alternatives to Self-Harm

Self-harm is a way that some teens deal with unpleasant feelings and difficult situations. In order to stop, you need to have effective, alternative ways of coping to be able to respond differently when you feel like harming yourself. For the time being, distractions are effective in the moment of allowing a sense of calm, and will keep you physically safe even when you are overwhelmed with the urge to self-harm.

Listed below are some alternatives to self-harm. Check those that you would be willing to try.

☐ Call a good friend.

☐ Chew something with a strong taste.

☐ Clean a room in your home.

☐ Compose a poem or letter to say what you feel.

☐ Contact an old friend.

☐ Crunch ice cubes.

☐ Dance with joy.

☐ Eat spicy foods.

☐ Exercise strenuously.

☐ Express your feelings in writing.

☐ Flatten a can and recycle it.

☐ Get to the gym and hit a punching bag.

☐ Go online to a self-help website.

☐ Jump rope.

☐ Listen to calming music.

☐ Massage your neck, hands, and feet.

☐ Meditate.

☐ Organize your office space.

☐ Paint, sculpt, or draw your feelings.

☐ Pet an animal.

☐ Count up to ten getting louder with each number.

☐ Plan an activity for your difficult time of day.

☐ Play a sport with gusto.

☐ Reach out to a trusted family member.

☐ Rip up junk mail.

☐ Run around the block.

☐ Scream into your pillow.

☐ Shred an already torn piece of clothing.

☐ Splash your face with cold water.

☐ Squeeze a stress ball.

☐ Stomp in heavy shoes.

☐ Suck on a lemon.

☐ Take a cold shower.

☐ Tear up a newspaper.

☐ Wrap yourself in a warm blanket.

☐ Write down negative feelings and then rip it up.

☐ Other _____

☐ Other _____

☐ Other _____

☐ Other _____

The 4 D's

When thinking about harming yourself, consider these four techniques that have been effective in helping teens overcome their self-harming urges.

These are referred to as the 4 D's: Delay, Distract, Divert, and Defuse. In the spaces that follow, describe how you could use each of these four techniques.

Ways to Overcome Self-Harm	An Example of How I Can Do This
Delay *(Example: Put off self-harm until I can talk with a support person.)*	
Distract *(Example: Go for a walk.)*	
Divert *(Example: Find an activity which has a similar effect to self-harm, but without causing me harm, like putting on loud music or dancing.)*	
Defuse *(Example: Deep breathing.)*	

© 2019 WHOLE PERSON ASSOCIATES, 101 WEST 2ND STREET, SUITE 203, DULUTH MN 55802 • 800-247-6789 • WHOLEPERSON.COM

How About Being Kind to Yourself?

One way to keep yourself in a positive state-of-mind is to find ways to be kind to yourself. We often become so busy, so preoccupied with everyday stuff, and so bogged down with the negatives that sometime surround us, that we forget to take care of ourselves.

Place a check in front of the feel-good items you will do for yourself when you feel the urge to injure yourself.

☐ Arrange to go to a movie with a friend.

☐ Attend a concert.

☐ Begin a new hobby.

☐ Blow bubbles.

☐ Catch up with a family member.

☐ Clean out a closet.

☐ Compose a letter to an old friend.

☐ Create a gratitude list.

☐ Curl up with a good light-reading book.

☐ Dig out your favorite game.

☐ Do deep breathing exercises.

☐ Donate money or goods to a charity.

☐ Enjoy the weather.

☐ Exercise at home.

☐ Express your love to someone special.

☐ Find quiet time.

☐ Finish something.

☐ Fix yourself a cup of hot tea.

☐ Get to the gym.

☐ Go bowling.

☐ Go shopping without spending a lot.

☐ Have fun with a pet.

☐ Hug someone you care about.

☐ Join a support group.

☐ Journal your feelings daily.

☐ Lie back and watch the clouds.

☐ Light a scented candle.

☐ Listen to a relaxation tape.

☐ Look up jokes or watch funny videos.

☐ Luxuriate in a bubble bath.

☐ Make an edible treat.

☐ Nap for ten minutes.

☐ Plan a dream vacation.

☐ Plant flowers.

☐ Play an instrument.

☐ Prioritize the things you need to do.

☐ Put flowers in your home.

☐ Reach out to a support person or group.

☐ Reflect on the positives in your life.

☐ Revisit a hobby that's been on hold.

☐ Ride somewhere special by bus, bike, or train.

☐ Sing or whistle a song.

☐ Sing along with music you love.

☐ Sit under a shady tree.

☐ Swim or splash in water.

☐ Take a walk in the rain.

☐ Use guided imagery.

☐ Visit the library.

☐ Walk through a park.

☐ Watch a sunrise or sunset.

☐ Water and care for indoor plants.

☐ Weed a garden.

☐ Window shop.

☐ Work on a jigsaw puzzle.

☐ Write creatively.

☐ Other _____

When you feel the urge to self-harm, take a look at this list again!

Let's Have Fun with Healthy and Unhealthy Self-Talk

Self-talk is the talk that goes on in your head. It's your inner voice, the way you talk to yourself. That talk can either be unhealthy *("I am a bad person." or "It was all my fault.")* or that talk can be healthy *("I am a darn good person!" or "I have a lot to offer others.")* In order to maintain a positive outlook, self-esteem, and overall well-being, you need to reduce your unhealthy self-talk and replace it with healthy self-talk.

Draw a picture of you holding your unhealthy self-talk words inside a bubble.

Now, draw a picture of you holding your healthy self-talk words inside a bubble.

Remember four important items:

1. Harming yourself and/or negative self-talk will never solve your problems – you have alternatives!
2. You can overcome and deal with your anger, sadness, and anxiety without harming yourself.
3. You need to continually remind yourself of your goodness.
4. You can accomplish this by posting your healthy self-talk pictures on your mirror or computer.

Quotes about Self-Harm

On the lines that follow, describe what each of these quotes means to you
and how each applies to YOUR life.

You should tell yourself frequently "I will only react to constructive
suggestions." This gives you positive ammunition against
your own negative thoughts and those of others.

~ **Jane Roberts**

_____

_____

_____

_____

In times of great stress or adversity, it's always best to keep busy,
to plow your anger and your energy into something positive.

~ **Lee Iacocca**

_____

_____

_____

_____

Once you replace negative thoughts with positive ones,
you'll start having positive results.

~ **Willie Nelson**

_____

_____

_____

_____

CHAPTER 2

Warning Signs

INTRODUCTION FOR THE CLINICIAN

People who are thinking about suicide will usually provide some clues and signs to those people around them. Sometimes these signs are very overt *(giving away possessions)* or they may be very subtle *(slowly withdrawing from other people)*. Suicide prevention starts with recognizing the various warning signs, taking them seriously, mobilizing a support system, and taking positive action.

Warning signs can be an indication that self-harm is prevalent or that the self-harm may be evidence of suicidal thoughts. Warning signs can also forewarn an <u>immediate risk</u> of suicide.

The person with these warning signs may desperately need your attention and your help:

  • Thoughts related to harming self.
  • Feelings people experience related to harming self.
  • Behaviors that indicate that a person may want to harm self.

Not every person who is considering suicide will talk about it, and not everyone who threatens suicide will follow through with it. However, every threat or warning sign of self-harm and/or suicide needs to be taken seriously.

This chapter will help you to help your clients take these actions:

  • Assess and explore warning signs and triggers.
  • Discover how thoughts, feelings, and actions are signs of suicidal ideation.
  • Explore life aspects that can provide hope for the future.

Warning Signs

Treatment Planning Options for Clinicians Working with Individuals and Small Groups.

Each item below is related to an assessment or activity page in the chapter and presents additional ways of adapting each exercise when working with individuals and/or small groups. They can be used at the discretion of the clinician prior to using the activity and can also be used to help participants process their learning related to the material covered on each page after using the handout.

50	*I Think About* Check-Up
Individuals	Respond to prompts and elaborate about thoughts that may indicate suicide warning signs.
Small Group	Discuss with clinician and peers and identify the trusted people with whom they will talk.
51	*My Emotions* Check-Up
Individuals	Respond to prompts and elaborate about their emotions that relate to suicide warning signs.
Small Group	Share with clinician and peers their three most intense emotions and the accompanying situations.
52	*My Behaviors* Check-Up
Individuals	Respond to prompts and elaborate about their behaviors that relate to suicide warning signs.
Small Group	Share with clinician and peers the behavior that concerns them the most; discuss alternative actions.
53	**Picturing My Pain**
Individuals	Draw a picture or caricature of one's emotional pain and identify a trusted person with whom to talk.
Small Group	Depict or describe in six words a positive emotion you want to experience; share with the group.
54	**Do You Feel Trapped?**
Individuals	Describe the circumstances surrounding feelings of being trapped and positive actions to take.
Small Group	Collaboratively create a fictional character who feels trapped and escapes in a healthy way.
55	**Triggering Thoughts**
Individuals	Identify personal and environmental stressors that may lead to self-injury impulses.
Small Group	Share one's most intense stressor; peers suggest positive ways to manage the situation and emotions.
56	**Why You Can Be Hopeful**
Individuals	Describe positive people and hopeful situations in one's life.
Small Group	**Hope-Bee:** Each participant shares information about a person who provides hope; next Bee: share ideas about a hopeful situation.
57	**You've Done It Before and You Can Do It Again!**
Individuals	Describe positive ways you managed a difficult situation, relationship, loss, and a big life change.
Small Group	Partners or panels discuss one of the items as group members observe and provide feedback.

(Continued on the next page)

Warning Signs *(Continued)*

Treatment Planning Options for Clinicians Working with Individuals and Small Groups.

58	**Let's Set Some POSITIVE Goals for the Future**
Individuals	Identify a personal or professional goal that gives meaning to life, and ways to achieve it.
Small Group	**Guess My Goal:** Share responses on the page except the top line *My Goal.* Peers guess the goal.
59	**Dealing with Emotions**
Individuals	Plan ways to avoid triggers, change thoughts and change responses to challenging situations.
Small Group	Each team responds to one prompt: Triggers, Change Thoughts, or Change Responses.
60	**My Life Needs Purpose**
Individuals	Complete sentence starters to discover your purpose that leads to fulfillment despite difficulties.
Small Group	Discuss or research people whose adversities have motivated them to help others.
61	**People Need Connections**
Individuals	Identify supportive people with whom to connect and ways they can help.
Small Group	Discuss the qualities that define a supportive person and ways to develop a support system.
62	**There ARE Alternatives**
Individuals	Discover untapped resources and develop coping skills by completing "I can ..." text boxes.
Small Group	"I can ..." Go 'Round: State positive alternatives to self-injury until no one can think of a new one.
63	**Self-Love**
Individuals	Note personal attributes one loves including those that may need some self-improvement.
Small Group	Compose self-talk phrases that show love while promoting changes in thoughts, feelings, and actions.
64	**When I Am Feeling Overwhelmed**
Individuals	Create a safety plan by removing possible methods of self-harm and naming support persons to call.
Small Group	Discuss ways to re-order priorities in your current dark situation to preserve life and hope.
65	**Thinking About It?**
Individuals	Respond "Yes" or "No" to indicators of a serious suicide plan; promise to talk with a trusted person.
Small Group	Anyone who responded "Yes" to one or more items meets with the clinician for further evaluation.
66	**A Quote About Warning Signs**
Individuals	Apply personally a quote that refers to suicide as a permanent solution to a temporary problem.
Small Group	Compose then share your own words of wisdom that promote life and hope even in difficulties.

Warning Signs

INTRODUCTION FOR THE PARTICIPANT

Warning signs can indicate that self-harm is prevalent or that the self-harmmay be evidence of suicidal thoughts. Warning signs can also indicate an immediate risk of suicide. Teens with these warning signs may desperately need attention and help.

Not every teen who is considering suicide will talk about it, and not everyone who threatens suicide will follow through with it; however, every threat or warning sign of self-harm and suicide should be taken seriously.

© 2019 WHOLE PERSON ASSOCIATES, 101 WEST 2ND STREET, SUITE 203, DULUTH MN 55802 • 800-247-6789 • WHOLEPERSON.COM

Suicide Warning Signs Check-Up
Directions

These three *Suicide Warning Signs Check-Ups*
are designed to assist you in identifying specific warning signs:

Check-Up #1 - I Think About
Check-Up #2 - My Emotions
Check-Up #3 - My Behaviors

Read each statement and decide how closely the statement describes you.

Place a check by the things you spend time thinking about.
You can write a comment on the lines next to each one if you choose.

Complete the bottom of each of the three scales

- This is not a test.
- There are no right or wrong answers.
- Do not spend too much time thinking about your answers.
- Be sure to read and check those that describe you.

(Turn to the next page and begin.)

I Think About Check-Up

Place a check by the things you spend time thinking about.
You can write a comment on the line next to each one if you choose.

I think about:

☐ Being a burden to my family _____

☐ Developing a suicide plan_____

☐ Dying can't be worse than I feel now _____

☐ Ending my pain _____

☐ Experiencing too much pain _____

☐ Feeling trapped_____

☐ Giving up _____

☐ Harming myself _____

☐ Having no purpose or meaning in my life_____

☐ How much emotional pain can I stand _____

☐ How much physical pain can I stand_____

☐ If anyone will care when I die _____

☐ Making preparations to die _____

☐ My financial troubles_____

☐ Not having a reason to live anymore _____

☐ Relying too much on my friends _____

☐ The fact that I have nothing to live for _____

☐ Ways I can die _____

☐ What will happen to the people I love _____

☐ Where people go when they die_____

☐ Whether I have already lost my friends _____

☐ Why do I need my possessions and who will receive them_____

Who are trusted professionals or people with whom you can discuss what you wrote on this page?
(Example: a mental health facilitator or medical professional; a positive support system or group;
a wise friend, family member, spiritual or religious leader, etc.) Use **name codes.**

_____

_____

_____

Are you willing to promise to talk with one or more of these people?_____ **When?** _____

Name_____**Date**_____

My Emotions Check-Up

Place a check by the emotions you feel.
You can write a comment on the line next to each one if you choose.

I am often feeling:

☐ Abusive _____

☐ Aggressive _____

☐ Agitated _____

☐ All alone _____

☐ Anger _____

☐ Anxiety _____

☐ Calm when I think of dying _____

☐ Empty _____

☐ Frustrated _____

☐ Hopeless _____

☐ Humiliated _____

☐ Intense mood swings _____

☐ Irritable _____

☐ Lonely _____

☐ Long-lasting sadness _____

☐ Nothing matters anymore, even me _____

☐ Overwhelmed _____

☐ Ready to explode, rage _____

☐ Shame _____

☐ Tired all the time _____

☐ Uninterested in most anything _____

☐ Unloved _____

☐ Unusually happy when I think of giving up _____

☐ Unwanted and/or unloved _____

Who are trusted professionals or people with whom you can discuss what you wrote on this page?
*(Example: a mental health facilitator or medical professional; a positive support system or group;
a wise friend, family member, spiritual or religious leader, etc.)* Use **name codes.**

_____

_____

_____

Are you willing to promise to talk with one or more of these people?_____ When? _____

Name_____ Date_____

My Behaviors Check-Up

Place a check by the behaviors to which you can relate.
You can write a comment on the line next to each one if you choose.

I am experiencing these behavior changes:

☐ Binging (food, alcohol, drugs, exercise, etc.)_____

☐ Constant crying_____

☐ Crabby, even to the people I care about _____

☐ Decreased concern about my cleanliness or self-care_____

☐ Desire to hurt myself _____

☐ Giving up on my personal and professional goals_____

☐ Handing out my possessions _____

☐ Hardly eating anything and then indulging excessively_____

☐ Having relationship issues_____

☐ Impulsive actions _____

☐ Increasing and/or beginning to abuse substances _____

☐ Isolating myself from people I care about_____

☐ Problems functioning at work _____

☐ Reckless reactions _____

☐ Reconnecting with old friends _____

☐ Sleeping way too much or way too little _____

☐ Slowly withdrawing from my usual activities _____

☐ Struggling to fall asleep _____

☐ Telling people goodbye in my own way _____

☐ Tidying up my personal affairs _____

☐ Trouble focusing and concentrating_____

☐ Wearing the same clothes for extended periods of time _____

☐ Withdrawing from family _____

Who are trusted professionals or people with whom you can discuss what you wrote on this page?
*(Example: a mental health facilitator or medical professional; a positive support system or group;
a wise friend, family member, spiritual or religious leader, etc.)* Use **name codes.**

_____

_____

_____

Are you willing to promise to talk with one or more of these people?_____ **When?** _____

Name_____**Date**_____

Picturing My Pain

Many teens feel extreme emotional pain with which they cannot seem to cope. The pain appears inescapable and will not go away. One way to gain control over the pain is to use your imagination and draw a picture or a caricature of what your emotional pain looks like to you.

Express yourself in the box below using pencil, markers, crayons, chalk, etc.

Who is a trusted professional or person with whom you can show and discuss your picture? *(Example: a mental health facilitator or medical professional; a positive support system or group; a wise friend, family member, spiritual or religious leader, etc.)* Use **name** codes.

_____

_____

_____

Are you willing to promise to talk with one or more of these people?_____ **When?** _____

Name_____ **Date**_____

Do You Feel Trapped?

Teens who are hurting and are contemplating harming themselves often feel trapped in their current situation without ways to escape the perceived trap.

Below, think about some of the ways that you feel trapped in your current situation and explore some ways to escape the perceived traps. Use Name Codes.

My Current Situation
Example: I was driving while drinking and hurt J.R.D. in another car.

Person/People
Example: J.R.D. is in the hospital.

Feelings
Example: Guilt, anger at myself, frustration, confusion.

Possible Actions
Example: Apologize to J.R.D. and his family. Enroll in a substance abuse program. Pay for damages.
Dedicate my life to talking to young people about the risks of drinking and driving.

Triggering Thoughts

Triggering happens when a certain event, sound, action by another person causes or triggers (sets off) a negative emotional response. The response can be fear, sadness, panic, flashbacks, pain, etc. Triggering thoughts tend to be personal or environmental stressors that put people at a higher risk for self-harm. Identifying the conditions or events that trigger your thoughts of harming yourself can be very important.

Below, identify some of the events or conditions that trigger negative thinking in you. Next to it, write why this is so. Some are listed for you. Write about your own triggers in the "Other" spaces below.

☐ Conflicts _____

☐ Failure _____

☐ Guilt _____

☐ Hopelessness _____

☐ Isolation _____

☐ No reason at all _____

☐ Pregnancy _____

☐ Severe illness _____

☐ Sexual identity _____

☐ Social embarrassment _____

☐ Substance abuse _____

☐ Transition or change _____

☐ Trauma anniversary date _____

☐ Other _____

☐ Other _____

☐ Other _____

☐ Other _____

Why You Can Be Hopeful

It is easy to dwell on the negatives in your life. Many teens who feel trapped in their current life often forget about the positive aspects of their lives. It is important to spend time thinking about the positive people in your life to remind yourself that you have a lot for which to be grateful, and in turn, to be hopeful.

Below, list some of the positive people in your life and describe why they can provide you with hope about your future if you let them!

Positive People In My Life	How This Person Provides Me With Hope	How I Can Hold Onto This Hope
Example: A new baby in our family.	B.J.R. and M.S.S. are great parents and I know he will grow up to be someone special. When he smiles, I smile.	I can try to hold on and not do anything rash. Meanwhile I can try to get some help for myself to be sure I get to all of his birthdays.

Below, list some of the hopeful situations in your life and describe why they can provide you with hope about your future if you let them!

Hopeful Situations In My Life	How This Situation Provides Me With Hope	How I Can Hold Onto This Hope
Example: I would like to become a nurse like my M.G.M..	I have a good chance of getting into an excellent college that is right in my town.	I will make a list of things I need to do to get good grades and look at every morning.

Who are trusted professionals or people with whom you can discuss what you wrote on this page?
(Example: a mental health facilitator or medical professional; a positive support system or group;

a wise friend, family member, spiritual or religious leader, etc.) _____

_____

_____

_____

You've Done It Before and You Can Do it Again!

Everyone has had difficult situations to overcome, relationships with people that have not worked out, loss of people or pets, and changes that seem overwhelming. There are times that they get through it and go forward. Let's focus on those difficult times in your life and ways you handled them well, even if it took a long time.

1. Name a **difficult situation** that happened in your life. _____
   _____

   Why were you proud of the way you handled this situation? _____
   _____

   What characteristics do you possess that helped get you through this difficult time? _____
   _____

2. Name a **relationship** that didn't work out as you had hoped. _____
   _____

   Why were you proud of the way you handled this situation? _____
   _____

   What characteristics do you possess that helped get you through this difficult time? _____
   _____

3. Name a **difficult loss** that happened in your life. _____
   _____

   Why were you proud of the way you handled this situation? _____
   _____

   What characteristics do you possess that helped get you through this loss?_____
   _____

4. Name a **big change** that happened in your life. _____
   _____

   Why were you proud of the way you handled this situation? _____
   _____

   What characteristics do you possess that helped get you through this change?_____
   _____

Let's Set Some POSITIVE Goals for the Future

Goals can provide you with hope, purpose, and meaning in life. When you begin to focus on a personal or professional goal, you become more engaged and feel more optimistic about your future.

It is important to set two goals for yourself: a personal goal (related to you and your relationships), professional goal (related to your work/volunteer life), and to work toward them. Each goal should be achievable or it will limit your motivation.

My Personal Goal: _____
_____
_____

Two or three small goals it will take to reach my personal goal: _____
_____
_____

Ways I will work toward my personal goal: _____
_____
_____

Why this personal goal matters to me: _____
_____
_____

How this personal goal will provide hope, purpose and/or meaning to me: _____
_____
_____

My Professional Goal: _____
_____
_____

Two or three small goals it will take to reach my professional goal: _____
_____
_____

Ways I will work toward my professional goal: _____
_____
_____

Why this professional goal matters to me: _____
_____
_____

How this professional goal will provide hope, purpose and/or meaning to me: _____
_____
_____

Dealing with Emotions

Emotions are a vital part of our everyday lives. Whether you are happy about a text message from a friend or feeling frustrated in rush hour traffic, the highs and lows you experience can significantly affect your daily attitude and internal well-being. Learning to deal with the wide range of positive and negative daily emotions is an important life skill to learn.

Ways to regulate your emotions.

Understand Your Triggers. Try to avoid circumstances that trigger unwanted emotions. *(Example: If you know that you are likely to get angry at the traffic when you drive a certain route, change your route.)*

What are two or three of your emotional triggers and how can you try to avoid them?

_____

_____

_____

Change Your Thoughts. At the core of your deepest emotions are the thoughts and beliefs that drive them. *(Example: You feel terribly sad and upset when you lose something.)*

By changing your thoughts, you may not be able to change the situation, but you can at least change the way you believe the situation is affecting you and how you feel about the situation. The best way to do this is to simply replace the negative thoughts that lead to unhappiness with thoughts that lead to joy or at least acceptance. Using the example above, *"I am sad because I lost my watch"* can be changed to *"I lost my watch, but it is only a thing. I can replace it. Everyone loses things from time to time!*

Using the spaces that follow, identify some of your negative thoughts about yourself and your situations. Then replace them with more positive, realistic thoughts:

Old Negative Thoughts	New Positive, Realistic Thoughts
_____	_____
_____	_____
_____	_____
_____	_____

Change Your Response. When you encounter things you cannot change, you can control your emotional responses to situations. Close your eyes in order to calm yourself down. Breathe in, count to five, and with your mouth closed, count as high as you can as you let the breath out through your nose. Paying attention to the counting will relax you! You can avoid emotional responses to your triggers. How and when will you do this?

_____

_____

_____

My Life Needs Purpose

Having a specific purpose in life can help you move on from the circumstances that are triggering negative emotions, thoughts, and behaviors. Purpose provides life with meaning when life seems meaningless. Purpose is what makes you feel fulfilled in life even when perceived negative things happen.

It is important that you have a purpose in and for your life. Respond to the following sentence starters.

My true purpose in life is ... _____

_____

_____

In my life, this has occurred and it validates my purpose ... _____

_____

_____

I was put on this earth to ... _____

_____

_____

I have the ability to ... _____

_____

_____

I can best help people by ... _____

_____

_____

I feel fulfilled when I ... _____

_____

_____

My present or future job, or my volunteer work, contributes to my life purpose in the following ways ...
My family contributes to my life purpose in the following ways ...

_____

_____

_____

Teens Need Connections

When teens feel down, feel like life has limited meaning, and/or feel stressed and trapped,
they often do not want to bother or be bothered by others.
THIS IS NOT A GOOD STRATEGY!
This is the time when it is vitally important to connect or reconnect with other people.

Complete the table below to identify new people with whom you can connect. These people may be family, friends, and professionals who can help you.

People I Want to Connect With **Use Name Codes**	Why	How It Can Help
Example: M.C.L – Her thirteen year-old dog died last month.	My twelve-year-old dog died a few days ago.	I am able to confide in her about my loss because she will understand how I feel.

Complete the table below to identify people with whom you can re-connect. These people may be family, friends, and professionals who can help you.

People I Want to Reconnect With **Use Name Codes**	Why	How It Can Help
Example: M.F.T. She was my therapist two years ago.	I need to talk with her. She was so helpful.	She is very caring and knows my background. She can help me get through this.

There ARE Alternatives

Some teens who are considering self-harm or suicide do so because they see these as the only two alternatives in the way they are living. It must be remembered that this type of all or nothing thinking can force them into poor decisions. It is important to remember that suicide or self-harm are not the only options.

In the boxes below, identify some of your untapped resources and coping skills possibilities. (Examples: Find a therapist with whom you 'click'; enter a support group; take a meditation class; use your logical personality to effectively solve problems; talk with a respected trusted person already in your life; try yoga; see a doctor and be honest, etc.)

I can ...

I can ...

I can ...

I can ...

I can ...

I can ...

I will promise to act on at least two of the items I wrote in the boxes within the next week.

Name_____ Date_____

Self-Love

Feeling good about yourself and loving yourself is critical in overcoming any overwhelming feelings and thoughts you may have about hurting yourself.

Self-love consists of the various ways that you love yourself. They might include your knowledge, personality, interests, characteristics, abilities, accomplishments, etc. It is also healthy to identify some of your areas for growth. You can love yourself even if you're clumsy, struggle with time management, etc. Self-love comes from loving your true self and trying to improve yourself.

In the shapes below, write words that describe some of the things you love about yourself.
Example: creative, hard-working, extroverted, knowledge of history, love for children, artist, great dog owner, good family member, logical, compassionate, etc.

When I Am Feeling Overwhelmed

Everybody needs a plan for those times when they feel overwhelmed by the stressors of life. This is particularly critical for people who might be thinking about self-injury or suicide.

You need to feel safe from hurting yourself and you need a concrete method for ensuring that you are safe. This can be accomplished by removing all potential weapons, limiting the amount of medicines available, avoiding reckless behavior, contacting a close friend, having a medical professional to confide in, etc.

Ways I Can Feel Safe	How This Will Help	Final Effect
Example: I can turn my Dad's gun in to the police station.	*I will know it is not available.*	*I will feel safer.*

Sometimes when you're overwhelmed by a situation – when you're in the darkest of darkness – that's when your priorities are reordered.

~ **Phoebe Snow**

What does the above quote mean to you?

_____

_____

_____

_____

Thinking About It?

One of the biggest warning signs is the creation of a plan for dying by suicide. The problem is that many teens do not realize they are taking steps to prepare for death before they hurt themselves. By completing this quick assessment, you can determine how much of a plan you consciously (or subconsciously) have completed.

After each sentence below, circle Yes or No to describe your behavior.

I have studied my family to identify a history of suicide.	Yes	No
I have stopped trying to avoid triggering conditions.	Yes	No
I have stopped thinking of positive alternatives.	Yes	No
I have been giving away some of my possessions.	Yes	No
I have said good-bye to some people.	Yes	No
I have a plan on how I will die by suicide.	Yes	No
I will no longer seek professional help.	Yes	No
I have started tying up loose ends.	Yes	No
I have updated my will recently.	Yes	No
I have written a suicide note for later use.	Yes	No

Even if you circled only one "Yes" answer, you may be at risk for hurting yourself.

Contact one or more of the following: a mental health facilitator or medical professional; a positive support system or group; a wise friend, family member, spiritual or religious leader. Use local or national resources and hotlines.

I promise to _____ by this day _____

Name _____ Date _____

A Quote About Warning Signs

On the lines that follow, journal about what this quote means to you and how it applies to YOUR life.

Suicide is a permanent solution to a temporary problem.

~ **Phil Donahue**

_____

_____

_____

_____

_____

_____

_____

_____

_____

_____

_____

_____

_____

_____

_____

_____

_____

_____

_____

_____

With whom will you share your completed page?

Suggestions: a mental health facilitator or medical professional; a positive support system or group; a wise friend, family member, spiritual or religious leader; local or national resources and hotlines, etc.

_____

_____

_____

© 2019 WHOLE PERSON ASSOCIATES, 101 WEST 2ND STREET, SUITE 203, DULUTH MN 55802 • 800-247-6789 • WHOLEPERSON.COM

CHAPTER 3

Risk Factors

INTRODUCTION FOR THE CLINICIAN

People who have suicidal ideation often experience the interplay of two unique sets of factors: **Risk Factors** and **Protective Factors.**

It is important to understand these sets of factors, be cognizant of both of them as you interact with and work with your clients, and recognize how they can affect the lives of your clients.

Risk Factors: A combination of individual, relational, career, community, and societal factors often contribute to the potential risk of suicide in clients. Risk factors are those characteristics associated with suicide, but they often are not the direct cause. Risk factors are biological, psychological, family, community, or cultural characteristics that tend to increase the possibility or probability that a self-harm or a suicide attempt or crisis will occur. This chapter will help clients explore their unique risk factors leading to suicidal ideation.

Protective Factors: A combination of factors that buffer people from suicidal thoughts and behavior. This chapter will include activities and reflection exercises to help your clients develop buffers to suicide.

This chapter will help you help your clients take these actions:

- Assess and explore the various risk factors in their lives.
- Become more aware of the factors that may be putting them at risk.
- Develop buffering and protective factors to strengthen their coping mechanisms and styles.

Risk Factors

Treatment Planning Options for Clinicians Working with Individuals and Small Groups.

Each item below is related to an assessment or activity page in the chapter and presents additional ways of adapting each exercise when working with individuals and/or small groups. They can be used at the discretion of the clinician prior to using the activity and can also be used to help participants process their learning related to the material covered on each page after using the handout.

72	**Risk Factors Insights**
Individuals	Respond to a list of Risk Factors by indicating "True" or "Not True" for oneself.
Small Group	Discuss individual risk factors in the group led by a clinician.
73	**Risk Factors Insights Clinical Impressions**
Individuals	Meet with the clinician and/or a trusted person as defined on the page.
Small Group	Discuss the qualities of supportive persons (empathy, etc.) versus non-supportive persons (judgmental, etc.).
74	**Coping Mechanisms**
Individuals	Respond to questions about internal and external coping mechanisms.
Small Group	Discuss recent changes in which they did or could have used positive coping skills.
75	**Has There Been a Recent Trauma?**
Individuals	Describe what occurred, one's reactions, positive and negative effects, what was learned, etc.
Small Group	Discuss reasons and ways to forgive self and others.
77	**Life Stressors**
Individuals	Depict or describe feelings about stressors regarding family, relationships, work, spare time.
Small Group	Share your stressors, peers give suggestions about ways to cope.
78	**Violence and Abuse**
Individuals	Describe the abuse suffered or ways you caused another to experience abuse and the effects.
Small Group	Discuss reasons people fear reporting abuse, why it must be reported, and how to report it safely.
79	**Make Your Home Safer**
Individuals	Identify ways to make your home safer from hazards that could lead to self-injury or suicide.
Small Group	Discuss places to avoid (high places, train tracks, traffic, etc.) where impulsivity could lead to death.
80	**My Family History**
Individuals	Describe family history regarding mental health, self-harm, abuse, and addiction issues.
Small Group	Discuss how you could cope without knowing your family history due to adoption, deaths, etc.

(Continued on the next page)

Self-Injury *(Continued)*

Treatment Planning Options for Clinicians Working with Individuals and Small Groups.

81	How Does Lifestyle Factor In?
Individuals	Respond to a list of lifestyle factors that can affect your ability to cope with a crisis.
Small Group	For each item, people who responded "A lot" give suggestions to others who responded differently.
82	Interacting and Isolating Myself
Individuals	Describe people you interact with often and whether and if one should continue or diminish future contact.
Small Group	Think of a list of qualities to look for in supportive people and qualities of people to avoid.
83	Impulsive Behaviors
Individuals	Describe your dangerous and reckless behaviors.
Small Group	Discuss the worst possible outcomes of impulsivity (harming others by accident; paralysis, etc.).
84	Hopefulness Assessment
Individuals	Respond to items related to your level of hopefulness about the future.
Small Group	Discuss responses with the clinician or in a small group led by the clinician.
85	Recent Losses
Individuals	Describe recent losses, their effects and impact on your ability to cope, and identify who can help.
Small Group	Discuss stages: denial, anger, bargaining, depression, acceptance, a "new normal," etc.
86	Effects of Contentment
Individuals	Complete sentences to describe what makes you content and ways to attain and maintain contentment.
Small Group	Create a list of challenging situations and ways to maintain contentment despite obstacles.
87	Effects of Sadness
Individuals	Describe circumstances and feelings related to sadness; identify ways to be more content.
Small Group	Discuss sad experiences that led to positive outcomes (a better relationship, a lesson learned, etc.).
88	Journaling about Risk Factors
Individuals	Personalize quotes about coping versus surviving, growth, change, losses, and treasures.
Small Group	Share stories about times difficulties turned out to be "blessings in disguise."

Risk Factors

INTRODUCTION FOR THE PARTICIPANT

Risk factors are biological, psychological, familial, community-based, or cultural characteristics that tend to increase the possibility or probability that self-harm, a suicide attempt, or a crisis will occur, or has occurred.

Risk Factors Insights
Directions

The Risk Factors Insights is designed to help you identify the specific risk factors that might increase the possibility or probability of self-harm, attempted suicide, or completed suicide.

This exercise contains 20 statements that include many of the risk factors related to self-harm and suicide.

Read each statement and decide if the statement is true for you or not true. If the statement is true, circle the number under the TRUE column, and if the statement is not true, circle the number under the FALSE column.

In the following example, the circled 2 indicates the statement is true for the Risk Factor Insights taker.

	TRUE	FALSE
I am currently unable to cope with life changes	(2)	1

This is not a test.
Since there are no right or wrong answers, don't spend too much time thinking about them. Your first reaction is usually the most accurate. Be sure to respond to every statement.

(Turn to the next page and begin.)

Risk Factors Insights

Read each statement and decide if the statement is true or false for you.
If the statement is true, circle the number under the TRUE column,
and if the statement is not true, circle the number under FALSE the column.
Be honest!

	TRUE	FALSE
I am currently unable to cope with life changes	2	1
I have a fairly stable life	1	2
I have a good support system	1	2
I have never tried to hurt myself in the past	1	2
I feel hopeless most of the time	2	1
I have thought about or developed a suicide plan	2	1
I do not abuse substances	1	2
I tend to be very impulsive	2	1
I have aggressive tendencies	2	1
I have people in my family who died by suicide	2	1
I have a history of being abused and/or abusing others	2	1
I have chronic illnesses and/or health problems	2	1
I do not stay sad or depressed for more than a day or two	1	2
I have experienced recent trauma that I cannot handle	2	1
I have recently received devastating news	2	1
I am too embarrassed to seek help	2	1
I have had a recent loss of a friend, pet, or family member	2	1
I do not have access to ways to die by suicide	1	2
I have isolated myself	2	1
I can't seem to find a way out of my problems	2	1

Give your completed Risk Factor Insights to your clinician who will discuss it with you.

Risk Factors Insights Clinician Impressions

The *Risk Factors Insights* is designed to measure some of the risk factors often associated with self-harm and suicidal behavior.

It should be noted that the appearance of **EVEN ONE** of these risk factor responses (circling the number 2) can increase the probability of self-injury or a suicidal crisis occurring.

As the number of risk factors on this assessment increases, so does the probability that a self-injury or a suicidal crisis might occur.

This indicates that the person completing the Risk Factors Insights needs to be in contact with one or more of the following:
- **a mental health facilitator or medical professional**
- **a positive support system or group**
- **a wise friend or family member**
- **a spiritual or religious leader**
- **hotlines to local or national resources**

Coping Mechanisms

Significant life events, whether positive or negative, can cause psychological stress. Teens who have experience in successfully coping with prior life changes, stressors, and crises are at a lower risk than those who lack critical coping mechanisms.

How do you cope with the stress? Journal below to explore how you use both internal and external coping mechanisms.

Write about a recently encountered change, crisis, or stressor with which you were able to successfully cope.

_____

_____

_____

How did you solve the problem? In retrospect, who could have helped you?

_____

_____

What family resources did you use? Did you ask any family members for help? In retrospect, could a family member have helped you?

_____

_____

_____

What are your social and community resources? Did you contact them for help?

_____

_____

_____

How were you able to cope using humor? Explain.

_____

_____

_____

Did you relax at all during this situation? If so, how did you relax? If you didn't, how could you have relaxed?

_____

_____

_____

Were you able to stay calm? If so, how? If not, what could you have done or who could you have called upon to help you stay calm?

_____

_____

_____

© 2019 WHOLE PERSON ASSOCIATES, 101 WEST 2ND STREET, SUITE 203, DULUTH MN 55802 • 800-247-6789 • WHOLEPERSON.COM

Has There Been a Recent Trauma

Thoughts of suicide are often related to major traumas teens have experienced in life. Think about any trauma you have experienced. Journaling about that experience can help you make meaning of the event and reduce your distress. Journal about your trauma below.

What happened? _____

_____

_____

_____

How did you react? _____

_____

_____

_____

To whom did you talk about it? _____

_____

_____

_____

Whom do you blame for what happened? _____

Is this valid? Why or why not?_____

_____

_____

_____

Were you able to forgive other people and yourself? Explain. _____

_____

_____

_____

(Continued on the next page)

Has There Been a Recent Trauma *(Continued)*

What, if anything, could you have done differently? _____

_____

_____

_____

How has this trauma affected your life in a positive way? _____

_____

_____

_____

How has this trauma affected your life in a negative way? _____

_____

_____

_____

How has the trauma changed your relationships with friends, family, loved ones, etc.? _____

_____

_____

_____

What have you learned about yourself because of this trauma? _____

_____

_____

_____

How have you grown or become stronger because of this trauma?_____

_____

_____

_____

Life Stressors

Major life stressors can be so extreme that they disrupt one's life in every way! These major life stressors *(rejection, divorce, failing an important test, breaking up with a boy or girl friend, financial crisis, disruptive life transitions, loss, etc.)* **can affect your ability to cope well.**

Identify some of your current life stressors and write or draw about how you are feeling about each of the four stressors.

Family Life	Relationships
School	Spare-Time

There's a lot of stress out there, and to handle it, you just need to believe in yourself; always go back to the person that you know you are, and don't let anybody tell you any different, because everyone's special and everyone's awesome.
~ **McKayla Maroney**

Violence and Abuse

Teens who have been subject to abuse in the past, or those who are currently being abused or who are experiencing violence, are particularly at risk for having self-harm and/or suicidal thoughts. They often see their situation as insurmountable and often see limited alternatives for resolution, although that probably is not true.

In the spaces below, write about your experiences of abuse and/or violence.

The Other Person (name code)	What Happened?	How It Affected Me	How It Affected the Other Person	How It Affected Our Relationship
Example: H.H.M.	He sexually abused me in my bedroom when I was five years old.	I didn't tell anyone because it would have broken up our family, I was terrified of him, had stomach aches, and told no one.	He didn't seem to be troubled at all. He spoke nicely to me but gave me knowing looks when no one was watching.	We have none!
Example: M.G.M.	I wasn't nice to her when we were growing up.	I avoided going anywhere with her. When we were alone I always spoke to her in a cruel way.	She wanted to have a good relationship but I didn't. She was sad and didn't know what she did wrong.	As I grew up I realized what I was doing, I apologized, she accepted it, and we have a fairly OK relationship now.

Tips for Overcoming Abuse in the Past

- Try to create closure and express what you could not express at the time. One way to do this is to write a letter to the person. You do not need to send it because the act of writing is the healing aspect of this technique.
- Talk about it with people in your support network.
- Be as mindful as possible and stay in the present. Set aside the past, live in the present, look forward and set goals for your future.

Make Your Home Safer

If you are experiencing suicidal thoughts or become worried that you might harm yourself in a rash moment when you are not thinking clearly, it is important to get rid of anything that you could use to harm yourself. These things might include alcohol, pills, knives, razors, or handguns. Give them to someone else for safekeeping, throw them out, or lock them away. Do not make it easy to change your mind.

What are some of the ways you will make your home safer?

Ways to
Make My
Home
Safer

If you do not feel safe staying by yourself at home, go to a place where you do feel safe.
(Example: a friend or family member's house, a community center, a hospital, or another public place.)

My Family History

A person's family history may be a determinant of being at risk for self-harm or a suicidal crisis.

Identify the issues that pretain to your family history that may be affecting your ability to cope, the family member that experienced the issue, and a description of the issue.

Family History Risk Factors	Family Member (name code)	The Family Member's Issue(s)
Example: Mental Health Issues	*M.G.F.*	*He had a severe depression. He wanted to die by suicide, and always threatened that he would, but he died of an illness.*
Mental Health Issues		
Suicide or Suicide Attempts		
Self-Harm		
Being Abused as an Adult or Child Physically, Sexually, Emotionally, Verbally, or Culturally		
Abusing an Adult or Child Physically, Emotionally, Verbally, Sexually, or Culturally		
Alcohol or Substance Abuse		
Other		

How does the awareness of your family history make you better able to cope with your own issues?

_____

_____

_____

How's Does Lifestyle Factor In?

One's lifestyle may be a major determinant in whether a suicidal crisis takes place. A lifestyle consisting of stable living conditions, a support network, and a job can help people to cope with a crisis that might lead to self-harm or suicidal ideations, feelings, or actions.

Complete the quick survey below to see how healthy your lifestyle is – or is not.

	A LOT	SOMETIMES	LITTLE/NONE
I have a job that I enjoy.	3	2	1
I have a stable family life.	3	2	1
I enjoy the company of friends.	3	2	1
I have the support of many people.	3	2	1
I am able to balance work and life.	3	2	1

Living TOTAL = _____

	A LOT	SOMETIMES	LITTLE/NONE
I eat a balanced diet.	3	2	1
I eat three healthy meals a day.	3	2	1
I eat healthy snacks rather than "junk" food.	3	2	1
I eat plenty of fresh fruits and vegetables.	3	2	1
I avoid fast food places.	3	2	1

Eating TOTAL = _____

	A LOT	SOMETIMES	LITTLE/NONE
I think pleasant thoughts when going to sleep.	3	2	1
I avoid drinking or eating too much caffeine before I go to sleep.	3	2	1
I try to get adequate amounts of sleep each night.	3	2	1
I am able to relax when I am stressed out before going to bed.	3	2	1
I take short naps when I need them.	3	2	1

Sleeping TOTAL = _____

	A LOT	SOMETIMES	LITTLE/NONE
I am able to relax fairly easily.	3	2	1
I like to relax outdoors and appreciate nature.	3	2	1
I breathe deeply when I begin to feel anxious.	3	2	1
I use basic calming exercises when I feel tense.	3	2	1
I think about enjoyable memories to help me relax.	3	2	1

Relaxing TOTAL = _____

	A LOT	SOMETIMES	LITTLE/NONE
I exercise several times each week.	3	2	1
I play sports, walk, or jog.	3	2	1
I get physical activity by working in the yard or garden.	3	2	1
I do aerobic exercises.	3	2	1
I love yoga or flexibility training.	3	2	1

Exercising TOTAL = _____

To score this quick evaluation of your current lifestyle, add the numbers you circled for each section.

Scores will range from 5 to 15 in each of the sections:

5 – 8   Your lifestyle will not be helpful in coping with life's stressors.

9 – 11   Your lifestyle and will be somewhat helpful in coping with life's stressors.

12 – 15   Your lifestyle will be very helpful in coping with life's stressors.

Interacting and Isolating Myself

Teens who continue to have regular social contact with many people are at a lower risk than those who have isolated themselves. These teens have others to offer emotional support, assistance with problem-solving, and resources to help deal with any immediate crisis. However, we are often better off having fewer or no relationships with people who de-energize us and who are negative forces in our life. We need to be sure we replace them with plenty of positive people in our lives who support us and allow us to support them!

Identify the people with whom you are continuing to interact.

People I Continue to Interact with Regularly (name codes)	What I Receive and What I Give in This Relationship	Is it a Good or Not so Good Thing that I Interact Regularly? Why?
Example: M.F.M.	*He is always supportive, always willing to listen. I do the same.*	*It's good! He's always there for me*
Example: B.G.S.	*She makes me miserable even though I try to do so much for her.*	*It's not so good! I feel obligated.*

Identify the people from whom you have withdrawn.

People From Whom I Have Withdrawn (name codes)	What Did I Receive and What Did I Give in This Relationship	Is it a Good or Not so Good Thing That I Have Withdrawn From This Contact? Why?
Example: M.F.M.	*I knock myself out for her but she is never there to support me.*	*It's good! I don't feel like I am being used.*
Example: B.G.S.	*He is a family member and tries to help but he's too negative.*	*It's not so good! I feel guilty. I will try to explain.*

Impulsive Behaviors

Engaging in deliberately impulsive and dangerous behaviors indicate risk for self-harm and/or suicidal ideation. These types of behaviors are considered an expression of intent to harm oneself. Teens who are in crisis tend to engage in impulsive and reckless behaviors such as speeding, abusing substances, abusing meds, unprotected sex, etc.

In the circles below, identify impulsive behaviors you engage in that are dangerous and reckless. Most important is to be honest with yourself by writing them below.

My Impulse Behaviors

Contact one or more of the following: a mental health facilitator or medical professional; a positive support system or group; a wise friend, family member, spiritual or religious leader, etc. to discuss your responses.

Hopefulness Assessment

Hope consists of a positive view of the future for yourself. Having hope is at the core of resiliency and the ability to bounce back while facing stress, crises, and/or unhealthy thoughts. Hopeful teens are able to feel at peace even when they confront suffering, pain, and disaster. Hope is important to sustain joy and happiness as you live your life.

This assessment contains 10 statements. Read each of the statements and decide whether or not the statement describes you. Circle the number of your response.

	YES	NO
When things go wrong, I remain hopeful	2	1
Most situations do not have a positive outcome	1	2
I usually see the positive side in most situations	2	1
I often feel as if my life is hopeless	1	2
I try to look on the bright side of things	2	1
I'm usually optimistic about my future	2	1
I am unhappy a lot of the time	1	2
I rarely get depressed when I think about the future	2	1
I seek out situations that make me happy	2	1
I often feel hopeless when anything in my life changes	1	2

TOTAL = _____

Add the numbers you circled and put that total on the TOTAL line. Then use the interpretation guide below to explore what your total means.

> Totals from 10 to 13 and indicate that you are not very hopeful about your future.
> Totals from 14 to 16 and indicate that you are somewhat hopeful about your future.
> Totals from 17 to 20 and indicate that you are hopeful about your future.

Contact one or more of the following: a mental health facilitator or medical professional; a positive support system or group; a wise friend, family member, spiritual or religious leader, etc., to support your effort to stay hopeful.

Recent Losses

Teens with few or no recent losses in life are at a lower risk for a crisis than those who have recently gone through losses. Losses might include such events as the loss of a parent or sibling, divorce, death of a friend, loss of a job, loss of a pet, or any other loss.

In the space that follows, journal about any recent losses you have experienced.

Your loss:

_____
_____
_____

What happened?

_____
_____
_____

How has this loss affected you?

_____
_____
_____

How has your life changed?

_____
_____
_____

How has this affected your ability to cope?

_____
_____
_____

Has this loss put you into a crisis? Describe the crisis.

_____
_____
_____

If you are in crisis, what actions are you going to take?

_____
_____
_____

Who can help you?

_____
_____
_____

Effects of Contentment

A high level of contentment can be a motivating factor to STOP your thinking about and considering self-harm or suicide.

In the top block below, write, draw, or cut pictures from magazines of three descriptors that make you content. In the bottom block, describe how you feel when you are content.
(Examples: peaceful, excited, cheerful, contented, joyful, encouraged, hopeful, etc.)

I am content when ...

1.

2.

3.

When I am content, I feel ...

1.

2.

3.

What can you do to be and stay content? _____

_____

_____

To support your efforts to stay content, contact one or more of the following: a mental health facilitator or medical professional; a positive support system or group; a wise friend, family member, spiritual or religious leader, etc.

 © 2019 WHOLE PERSON ASSOCIATES, 101 WEST 2ND STREET, SUITE 203, DULUTH MN 55802 • 800-247-6789 • WHOLEPERSON.COM

Effects of Sadness

A high level of sadness can be a motivating factor to CONTINUE your thoughts of self-harm or suicide.

In the top block below, write, draw, or cut pictures from magazines of three descriptors that make you sad. In the bottom block below, describe what other feelings you have when you are sad. (Examples: sleepy, mood swings, no appetite, irritability, no energy, negative, depressed, no contentment, no interest, feel hopeless, feel empty, critical.)

I am sad when ...

1.

2.

3.

When I am sad, I feel ...

1.

2.

3.

What can you do or who can you talk with to stop being sad and be more content with your life?

_____

_____

To support your efforts to stop being sad, contact one or more of the following: a mental health facilitator or medical professional; a positive support system or group; a wise friend, family member, spiritual or religious leader, etc.

Journaling about Risk Factors

On the lines that follow, describe what each of these quotes means to you and how each applies to YOUR life.

I choose not to think of my life as surviving, but coping.

~ Lorna Luft

_____

_____

_____

_____

_____

_____

_____

_____

_____

_____

The garden is growth and change and that means loss as well as constant new treasures to make up for a few disasters.

~ May Sarton

_____

_____

_____

_____

_____

_____

_____

_____

_____

_____

CHAPTER 4

Prevention

INTRODUCTION FOR THE CLINICIAN

Self-harm and suicide can often be prevented. By noticing the warning signs and risk factors, you can help your clients prevent self-harm and suicidal thoughts.

Many different types of preventive techniques are designed to help your clients cope with their issues, deal effectively with stress, and find hope for the future. These self-harm and suicide prevention techniques are meant to help people learn effective skills for dealing with life stressors and reducing the probability of harming themselves.

Techniques used in the prevention of suicide are designed to help your clients look forward to their future, develop and maintain hope that the future will be better, develop mindfulness so that thoughts do not trigger negative emotions, and build stress-reduction factors like maintaining a healthy lifestyle and developing effective coping mechanisms.

This chapter will help you to help your clients to take these actions:

- Assess and explore how equipped they are for managing life's stressors.
- Explore some of the factors that can lead to prevention.
- Practice some methods for relieving stress and finding hope.

Prevention

Treatment Planning Options for Clinicians Working with Individuals and Small Groups.

Each item below is related to an assessment or activity page in the chapter and presents additional ways of adapting each exercise when working with individuals and/or small groups. They can be used at the discretion of the clinician prior to using the activity and can also be used to help participants process their learning related to the material covered on each page after using the handout.

93	*Self–Reflection Survey* Directions
Individuals	Respond to items that reflect reasons to live, coping skills, monitoring thoughts and self-talk.
Small Group	Review responses with the clinician or group led by clinician.
94	**Self–Reflection Survey**
Individuals	Clinician evaluates each person's results and refers those in need of a more intense level of care.
Small Group	Discuss survey with the clinician and peers the insights gained from it.
95	**Clinician's Process for Analyzing the *Self-Reflection Survey***
Individuals	Clinicians discuss the survey descriptions with each participant; plan ways to meet identified needs.
Small Group	Discuss with the clinician and peers the ways to find purpose, cope, and change negative self-talk.
96	**My Reasons to Keep on Going**
Individuals	Identify who and what one cares deeply about, describe the reasons for and benefits of caring.
Small Group	Imagine and discuss a list of reasons that could be in the "Other" category.
97	**Positive Distractions**
Individuals	Describe positive distractions that have helped in the past.
Small Group	Discuss distractions they have not tried but sound appealing and are doable.
98	**My Bucket List**
Individuals	Identify positive activities one wants to engage in and ways to accomplish them.
Small Group	Share their most important bucket list item; peers suggest ways to make the accomplishment possible.
99	**Coping Strategies**
Individuals	Describe ways to use awareness of triggers, deep breathing, exercise, and hobbies to calm oneself.
Small Group	Volunteers lead a discussion of triggers, exercise, hobbies, and demonstrate deep breathing.
100	**Being Mindful**
Individuals	Describe what prompts one to dwell on the past, and then discuss ways to stay in the present and let go of the past.
Small Group	Discuss ways to explore the outdoors, meditate, journal, and enjoy satisfying moments.

(Continued on the next page)

Prevention (Continued)

Treatment Planning Options for Clinicians Working with Individuals and Small Groups.

101	**My Healthy Lifestyle**
Individuals	Evaluate the client's healthy and unhealthy dietary and sleep habits based on the page's information.
Small Group	Discuss ways to eat healthy foods if there is little time to cook and a tight budget.
102	**Problem Solving**
Individuals	Describe a current problem. Brainstorm possible solutions then choose the best resolution.
Small Group	Share a problem. Peers explore possible solutions. Discuss pros and cons of each.
103	**Unhealthy Coping**
Individuals	Using a list of category prompts, have participant note unhealthy ways of coping he or she uses, why they use that method, and what the effects can be when used.
Small Group	Discuss reasons and the detrimental effects of pretending and/or lying to people.
104	**Healthy Coping**
Individuals	Using a list of category prompts, note healthy ways of coping, reasons, and the effects.
Small Group	Discuss ways to take control of their own lives and what is beyond their personal control (what others do, etc.)
105	**Journaling Your Feelings**
Individuals	Instruct the client to journal about his or her feelings each day for one week.
Small Group	Discuss other creative ways to express feelings: write poetry or lyrics; play music; draw or paint, etc.
106	**Challenge Negative Thoughts**
Individuals	Write two sets of negative feelings, the triggering thoughts, and resultant behaviors.
Small Group	Board Activity: Change negative thoughts to positive and note resultant feelings and behaviors.
107	**Change Negative Thinking**
Individuals	List negative thoughts and then change each one to a more positive but realistic thought.
Small Group	Cut out the negative thought boxes. Distribute and have participants write down a negative thought. Collect. Peers pull a cutout, read aloud, and change it to a positive.
108	**Quotes About Suicide Prevention**
Individuals	Personalize two quotations about suicide prevention.
Small Group	Compose their own words of wisdom, compile a list, and distribute photocopies or electronically.

Prevention

INTRODUCTION FOR THE TEEN PARTICIPANT

Self-harm and suicide prevention techniques are designed to help you learn effective skills for dealing with life stressors and reducing the probability of harming yourself.

Self-Reflection Survey

Directions

The Self-Reflection Survey has 18 statements

Read each of the statements and decide whether the statement describes you or not.

EXAMPLE:

If the statement does describe you, check the circle in front of the sentence.

✔ I continue to have an interest in my usual activities.

If the statement does not describe you, put an x in the circle.

✗ I continue to have an interest in my usual activities.

This is not a test.
Since there are no right or wrong answers, do not spend too much time thinking about your answers.
Be sure to mark each statement with a check or x. Be honest!

(Turn to the next page and begin.)

Self-Reflection Survey

Place a check next to the statements that are true for you and place an x for the statments that are not true for you.

#1

○ I continue to have an interest in my usual activities.

○ I have a lot to look forward to.

○ I care what happens to me.

○ I like spending time with anyone I love.

○ I have a lot of people who care about me.

○ I am able to see things in a positive way.

#2

○ I am able to deal with stressful situations.

○ I manage my life effectively.

○ I can see my way out of my situation.

○ I am eating and sleeping well.

○ I am able to go to work and function.

○ I cope with my negative feelings.

#3

○ I feel like I am a worthwhile human being.

○ I believe things in my life will get better.

○ I never feel like a failure.

○ I like being a help to my loved ones.

○ I am able to stop the negative thoughts in my head.

○ I feel pretty good most all of the time.

© 2019 WHOLE PERSON ASSOCIATES, 101 WEST 2ND STREET, SUITE 203, DULUTH MN 55802 • 800-247-6789 • WHOLEPERSON.COM

Process for Analyzing the *Self-Reflection Survey*

It is important for you to know the status of your clients reasons to keep going, or not!

It is important to help clients reflect on their reactions to three critical aspects of preventing self-harm and suicide.

    1 - Find reasons to live.
    2 - Learn effective coping mechanisms.
    3 - Monitor and manage self-talk and thoughts that can lead to negative emotions.

• In each of the sections on the previous page, count the sentences that had an X.

• Then, transfer the totals to the space below:

    1. = **Reasons to Live**   Total = _____

    2. = **Coping**   Total = _____

    3. = **Self-Talk**   Total = _____

You may feel that this process helped you learn more about the client, and feel it is unnecessary to discuss the scores with the participant(s). However, you may want to talk to the person or ask why they put an X on a certain item(s).

Survey Descriptions – For Clinicians Only

1. **Reasons to Live** – People who placed several X marks on the survey may have lost interest in people and activities and feel that they have nothing to look forward to.

2. **Coping** – People who placed several X marks on the survey may be having trouble coping with challenges in life, struggling with problem solving, and trying to cope with unfinished business.

3. **Self-Talk** – People who placed several X marks on the survey may be experiencing negative emotions that are being driven by negative self-talk, and they are unable to monitor and manage these thoughts.

My Reasons to Keep on Going

When your life is negative, it is important to reflect on the people and things you love in life. This can include family members you love, friends you care deeply about, places you enjoy visiting, music, movies, your favorite foods, and sports. Use Name Codes.

In the spaces that follow, list some of your reasons that tell you to "keep on going."

My Reasons to Keep on Going	Why This is Important to Me	How This Will Help Me
Example: Family J.A.F.	*I enjoy going to basketball games with him. We usually talk about everything.*	*I feel like I can say anything to him when we are alone together.*
Example: Family M.D.R.	*MDR is expecting a baby*	*I want to see my niece and watch her grow up.*
Family		
Good Friends		
Community		
Love to Learn		
Travel		
Special Occasions		
Trust that things will get better		
Other		
Other		

Positive Distractions

It is important to have positive distractions that you can engage in daily to distance yourself from negative thoughts of harm when life seems particularly challenging. Think about some positive distractions that have worked in the past.

(Examples: eat at your favorite restaurant, connect with an old friend, read a mystery book, garden, walk in the woods, write your story.)

Now you list your own.

My Positive Distractions

My Bucket List

Most people have a bucket list (unfinished business). A bucket list consists of those things you wish you had finished, or could spend more time doing. It is an ongoing process and never really completed. There are always infinite possibilities to look forward to seeing and doing.

(Examples: finding places to travel, reconnecting with old friends, discovering a business you want to begin, volunteering at a certain place, planting a tree and watching it grow, learning to ballroom dance, running a marathon, going up in a hot air balloon, swimming with a dolphin, attending a concert, getting a star's autograph, etc.)

Identify your unfinished business. (Bucket List)

On My Bucket List	Why This Sounds So Appealing	Ways I Can Make This Happen!

This is the most optimistic I've been in a long time.
I've got some unfinished business.

~ Sterling Marlin

Coping Strategies

There will be days when it is really difficult to cope with the problems and challenges that life throws at you. When you are anxious, depressed, tense, or upset, it becomes even more difficult to cope effectively. However, it is possible to learn some coping strategies that you can use to calm yourself when you are feeling that way.

The following coping strategies will help you deal with thoughts of harming yourself should they occur.

Triggers: Be aware of triggers *(Examples: birthdays, anniversaries, holidays, locations, people, fragrances, foods, etc.)* that may cause strong feelings. This awareness will help you to be more emotionally prepared. What are your triggers?

_____

_____

_____

Deep Breathing: When you are feeling sad, it is important to remember to keep breathing. The deeper you can breathe, the better. Try deep breathing when you find yourself feeling upset or sad. Start by inhaling deeply, hold it to a count of five, and then exhale slowly to a count of eight or more. Count your breaths in and out. By counting your breaths, your mind shuts off and reduces any negative thoughts that might be going through your head. Repeat this several times. Describe how it feels.

_____

_____

_____

Exercise: When you are having negative thoughts of hurting yourself in any way, think about exercising. This can help reduce your negative thinking and eliminate increased stress hormones in your body. It will be helpful to get your body accustomed to exercise if you have not been exercising regularly. Describe your current exercise regimen and how you can increase it.

_____

_____

_____

Hobbies: Make time to do something you have always enjoyed. *(Example: art work, dancing, singing, cooking, playing chess, reading, camping, swimming, playing the guitar, etc.)* What are some new hobbies you can consider?

_____

_____

_____

Being Mindful

Mindfulness: Those calm and quiet moments when you stay in the present, not thinking about the past or future at all. This allows you to reconnect to self, to increase the ability to use your senses, and to make thoughtful decisions.

When you are feeling sad or upset, the smallest stressor can ignite thoughts that can make you feel you just cannot go on. At this point, you may experience unexpected emotions and irrational thinking. Using mindfulness techniques, *(engage in deep breathing, explore the outdoors, meditate, journal, enjoy the satisfying moments, stay positive, etc.)* people are able to focus their attention in the present and observe what goes on around them without judging anything. This can help to reduce the strong emotions that accompany irrational thinking before it affects you.

Think about some of the times when you tend to dwell on the past. Use Name Codes when describing other people.

When I Tend to Dwell on the Past	What Prompts Me to Dwell on the Past	How I Can Stay Present and Let it Go
Example: When M.S.A. criticizes me for being negative. I start bringing up all the times she never had anything good to say about me.	*I become furious. She has always criticized me, even when I was feeling positive. I do not want her feedback at all.*	*I just need to walk away! I will go outside and smell the fresh air and notice the flowers. I will come back in and change the subject.*

My Healthy Lifestyle

One of the ways to cope with sadness and thoughts of harming yourself is to work on having a healthy lifestyle. This will help reduce some of your current stress, and subsequently build resilience against future stressors.

Suggestions for a Healthy Food Lifestyle

Your body needs to be healthy in order to fight off the effects of stress and sadness. Stress is a bodily reaction to anything that interferes with your daily functioning. An effective diet can help you fight stress and sadness.
- Decrease both your caffeine and alcohol intake. Alcohol and caffeine both can increase stress response in people. Water has been shown to be healthy and a reliever of stress.
- Eat healthy by having smaller meals throughout the day as opposed to eating three really large meals. Reduce fried and "fast foods." Eat fewer carbs and less sugar.

My Healthy Dietary Habits	My Unhealthy Dietary Habits

Suggestions for a Healthy Sleep Lifestyle

It is important to get enough sleep, but not too much sleep, so that your body functions at its highest capacity. Sleep allows your body to rest and reduce the symptoms of stress and sadness; poor sleep can actually worsen existing stress. However, sleeping too much to escape from your feelings, or because of low energy and lack of motivation, is not helpful.
- By sticking to a specific sleep schedule you will develop a natural sleep rhythm. You will feel tired at bedtime and energized in the morning.
- Choose a relaxing bedtime ritual that you engage in away from bright lights, loud noises, and strenuous activities. You might read a book, do a crossword puzzle or listen to soothing music. Avoid watching television and using technology at least one hour before bedtime. Ensure your bedroom is dark and cool.
- When you close your eyes, and unhappy thoughts enter your mind, deep breathe to a count of 5 and let go of that breath while you count. This will take your mind off of those thoughts and can put you to sleep after you do this several times. It may help to repeat a positive phrase as you breathe. (Example: "Peace in; Stress out.")
- Music can help too!

My Healthy Sleep Habits	My Unhealthy Sleep Habits

Problem Solving

Teens who are troubled and sad, who cannot solve their problems, often have thoughts of harming themselves. This inability to solve problems magnifies their idea that their problems are insurmountable. The opposite is often true, given the right problem-solving skills. It is important to develop a system for solving small or large problems.

Identify and write about one of your problems._____

_____

Who is involved? _____

_____

What happened? _____

_____

How is this problem affecting you?_____

_____

Brainstorm three possible solutions to your problem. Don't judge your ideas, don't say the solutions won't work, just identify them and write them down.

1. _____

   _____

2. _____

   _____

3. _____

   _____

Ask a trusted person to discuss the above three solutions with you.

With a mental health facilitator or medical professional; a positive support system or group; a wise friend, family member, or a spiritual or religious leader; read your three solutions and answer the following questions to identify the best choice.
  • Discuss the pros and cons of each of these solutions.
  • Which one is the most feasible?
  • Do you have the ability to carry the solution out?
  • Can the solution be implemented? If so, how?

Which solution provides you with the best chance of success: 1, 2, or 3? Why this solution?

_____

_____

_____

Unhealthy Coping

When you feel sad, angry, guilty, emptiness, grief, etc., you may feel there is nothing that can change the situation. Unfortunately, many people resort to coping in unhealthy ways to deal with their pain.

In the table below fill out columns two and three for those unhealthy coping skills that apply to you. Be honest!

Unhealthy Ways I Cope	Why I Do It	How It Affects Me
Example: Alcohol	*Alcohol dulls my pains and makes me sleepy. I fall asleep and forget.*	*Sometimes it leads to impulsive behaviors that I later regret.*
Alcohol or Tobacco		
Drugs		
Eating		
Gambling		
Pretending or Lying to My Loved Ones		
Shopping, Spending Money		
Unprotected Sex		
Watching Television or on Social Media All Day		
Isolating Myself		
Other		

Healthy Coping

When you feel sad, angry, guilty, shame, emptiness, grief, etc., you may feel there is nothing that can change the situation, but there is! There are healthy ways to cope! .

In the table below, respond to the items in the first column that apply to you. Be honest!

Healthy Ways I Cope	Why I Do It	How It Affects Me
Example: Completely avoid caffeine, alcohol, and nicotine.	*I used it to fit in but found I really didn't need it anymore.*	*I enjoy nature. I take walks outside with a friend I can talk to.*
Completely Avoid Caffeine, Alcohol, and Nicotine.		
Create A Support System of Trusted People. Talk to an Appropriate Person When Needed.		
Get Enough Sleep. Not Too Much. Not Too Little.		
Indulge in Physical Activity.		
Manage Your Time Well.		
Say No to Someone Else, or to YOURSELF, if You Know it's Wrong.		
Try Relaxation Methods.		
Take Control of Your Life. Don't Allow it to Take Control of You.		
Make Time for Loved Ones.		
Other		

Journal Your Feelings

Teens with harmful or suicidal thoughts often experience a wide variety of emotions. It is important to find ways to express these emotions so they are not bottled up inside of you. One way to express your feelings is through a feelings journal. Writing about your experiences can help you recognize and acknowledge what you are feeling.

Below, journal about the feelings you experience this week. If you find this helpful, continue to do it every week. You do not need to share your journal if you choose not to. If you do, it may help people close to you understand what you are feeling.

Day	How I Felt About My Day
Sun.	
Mon.	
Tues.	
Wed.	
Thurs.	
Fri.	
Sat.	

What trends do you see? _____

_____

_____

Which was your best day, and why?_____

_____

_____

Challenge Negative Thoughts

If you are thinking negative thoughts about what to do to put yourself at peace, negative thinking is probably not helping your pain and could possibly be the source of your pain. People tend to operate from a thinking perspective. This means that your thinking (often negative) can promote and escalate certain behaviors and emotions. For example, if you think to yourself something like this: *I hate myself. I said such stupid things,* you will probably feel sad. However, if you then say to yourself "I will never do that again!" and you carry that out, you will probably feel better. Emotions are often generated by what you think. The use of positive thinking will have the opposite effect and help you to feel better.

Think about two recent times when you experienced a negative emotion. Identify your negative emotion in the top box, identify the thinking that prompted the emotion in the second box, and identify any behavior that followed as a result in the third box.

Emotion

Thought

Behaviors

Emotion

Thought

Behaviors

Change Negative Thinking

Your emotions are created from your thinking. If you are thinking positively, your emotions will be positive. On the other hand, if you have negative thoughts, you will have negative emotions. For example, if you think "I am a bad person" you will feel sad.

On the left side, identify some of the negative thoughts that you are having. On the right side, turn that negative thought into a positive one.

Negative Thoughts	More Positive Thoughts
Example: I am worthless to everyone.	My family loves me, even when I am miserable. The people at work think I do a great job. My dog likes me best of anyone in the family! I am not worthless to everyone!

If you have a difficult time completing the second column, ask a trusted person for help. This process will allow you to have more positive emotions.

Quotes About Suicide Prevention

On the lines that follow, describe what each of these quotes means to you
and how each applies to YOUR life.

Never give up for that is just the place and time that the tide will turn.
                                          ~ Harriet Beecher Stowe

_____

_____

_____

_____

_____

_____

_____

_____

To anyone out there who's hurting – it's not a sign of weakness
to ask for help. It's a sign of strength.

                                          ~ Barack Obama

_____

_____

_____

_____

_____

_____

_____

_____

© 2019 WHOLE PERSON ASSOCIATES, 101 WEST 2ND STREET, SUITE 203, DULUTH MN 55802 • 800-247-6789 • WHOLEPERSON.COM

CHAPTER 5

Support

INTRODUCTION FOR THE CLINICIAN

It takes a team to help teens who are harming themselves or thinking about dying by suicide. This type of social support is critical in helping teens through the stressful times that can trigger suicidal ideation.

Support refers to anyone, or any place that can provide teens with personal, social, physical, and emotional support. It is necessary to remind your clients that it is important for them to seek out and accept support, whether they think they need it or not.

Family members, friends, helping professionals and other caregivers are very critical to suicide prevention and can be involved in many ways. A support system can help increase the protective factors in a person's life and can also provide support during a suicidal crisis, encourage clients to seek and adhere to a treatment program, and help keep the person safe during periods of crisis.

This chapter will help you to help your clients to take these actions:

- Assess and explore their level of support.
- Create plans for seeking and accepting help.
- Reflect and identify specific people who can be part of their social support system.

Support

Treatment Planning Options for Clinicians Working with Individuals and Small Groups.

Each item below is related to an assessment or activity page in the chapter and presents additional ways of adapting each exercise when working with individuals and/or small groups. They can be used at the discretion of the clinician prior to using the activity and can also be used to help participants process their learning related to the material covered on each page after using the handout.

113	**A Support System Review**
Individuals	Indicate "True" or "Not True" on a checklist to evaluate one's current support system.
Small Group	Share one's Support System Review with the clinician or in a group led by the clinician.
114	**Clinician's Process for Evaluating A Support System Review**
Individuals	Clinician helps evaluate one's support system and explains concepts noted on the page.
Small Group	Discuss experiences with people who seemed supportive but were not wise with their advice.
115	**Crisis Treatment Goals**
Individuals	Create treatment goals using a list of prompts and identify ways to reach the goals.
Small Group	Create a list of emotional strengths. Take turns sharing how one does or could exemplify each.
116	**My Support Team**
Individuals	List supportive people in each category: Medical, Mental Health, Family/Friends, Spiritual.
Small Group	The CONTRACT: Peers suggest ways to find supportive people for those whose lists are limited.
117	**My Changes**
Individuals	From a list of prompts, identify changes, their effects, and ways to reduce related stress.
Small Group	Discuss types of changes that could be in the "Other" category and ways to reduce related stress.
118	**My Emergency Plan**
Individuals	Write contact info for support people, providers, spiritual leaders, and list current medications.
Small Group	Discuss what it means to sign a contract; talk about the importance of upholding a promise.
119	**My Warning Signs**
Individuals	Write one's warning signs on a circular graphic.
Small Group	Share stories of times that recognizing a warning sign potentially saved a life.
120	**What My Situation Looks Like**
Individuals	Show what a current difficult situation looks like, then show how it would look if one made it better.
Small Group	Share one's situation. Peers brainstorm ways to work it out or make it better.

(Continued on the next page)

Support *(Continued)*

Treatment Planning Options for Clinicians Working with Individuals and Small Groups.

121	**Support from Others**
Individuals	Note support people and the types of additional help one wants them to provide.
Small Group	Role play asking people for specific help, or compose and read aloud a note to give to them.
122	**Controlling Those Feelings**
Individuals	Compare circumstances and people present when one experienced negative and positive emotions.
Small Group	Give examples of times negative or positive thoughts fueled negative or positive feelings.
123	**A Safety Agreement**
Individuals	Document the dangerous behaviors one will avoid; promise to seek help if impulses arise.
Small Group	Discuss the impact of substances on impulsivity and the potential value of appropriate meds.
124	**Let's Celebrate**
Individuals	Plan positive reinforcements to enjoy with one's support team and individually.
Small Group	Imagine feeling proud. Participants share visions of what they will be doing when living a healthy lifestyle.
125	**Find or Start a Support Group**
Individuals	Read the text. Research and document contact information for a support group in one's area.
Small Group	Discuss support group experiences; all groups are not the same; it takes time to find the right "fit."
126	**Quotes about Support**
Individuals	Apply two quotations to one's life detailing ways to implement the wisdom.
Small Group	Compose and share one's own words of wisdom and/or research other quotations about support.

Support

INTRODUCTION FOR THE PARTICIPANT

Support refers to anyone or any place that can provide teens with personal, social, physical, and emotional support.

It is important for you to seek out and accept support, whether you think you need it or not.

A Support System Review

The *Support System Review* is designed to help you review how much support you feel you have in your life. This support can come from your family, friends, professionals, community facilities, online websites, etc.

For each of the statements, circle the number under the column that best describes you. If the statement is TRUE, circle the number under the TRUE column. If the statement is NOT TRUE, circle the number under the NOT TRUE column.

	TRUE	NOT TRUE
When it comes to my self-injury or suicidal thoughts ...		
I have a helpful support system	2	1
I have people in my life who help me cope	2	1
I have access to mental health professionals	2	1
I regularly participate in a support group	2	1
I have a crisis plan in place	2	1
I have family members in whom I confide	2	1
I am in touch with a spiritual or religious leader	2	1
I have friends who listen to me no matter how often I need them	2	1
I know of community resources I can access	2	1
I have people who give me positive reinforcement	2	1
I am open to finding more supportive people in my life	2	1
I like to support other people when they have problems	2	1
I would be willing to try to find someone to start a support group	2	1
I keep a list of names and phone numbers of supportive people	2	1
I keep a list of places with phone numbers if I need help	2	1
I am not embarrassed to ask for help if I need it	2	1
I know people who will listen when I need to talk	2	1

COMBINED TOTAL = _____

A Clinican's Process for Evaluating a Support System Review

This page is meant to help your clients review how much support they feel they have access to every day in life, as well as in times of crisis.

Profile Interpretation

The higher the score, the better the client's support system is, and the more support they have access to. Remind the client to reach out to all of the people in their support system when they feel isolated, angry, unable to cope, etc.

Emphasize the fact that many people who are supportive are not always wise in their advice. If they are not being helpful in a positive way, the person needs to find others who will be!

If the score is lower than the participant thought it would be, it is critical to process the results with the person and create a plan for developing a more effective support system.

These people or sources are excellent supports!

*A mental health facilitator or medical professional;
a positive support system or group;
a wise friend, family member, spiritual or religious leader, etc.*

Local or national resources and hotlines. (see page 140)

Crisis Treatment Goals

People in crisis, especially those who are having self-harm or suicidal thoughts, need treatment goals to provide a safety net for the present, as well as security in the future. Treatment plans usually require people to set goals for their needs and explore how they will reach these goals.

My Primary Issue:_____

Complete the following table to create your treatment goals.

Treatment Aspects	My Goals	Ways I Can Reach This Goal
Example: Recognize My Warning Signs	*I need to be more aware of the times when my behavior suddenly changes.*	*Be more present and more aware of what my body is telling me.* *Call a support person immediately.*
Recognize My Warning Signs		
Lack of Ability to Cope with _____		
Rely on My Strengths		
Overcome My Weaknesses		
Confide in my Supportive Relationships		
Feel Hopeful		
Other		

My Support Team

It is very important to have a team of people who can be activated when a person is considering self-harm or suicide. This support team can help provide answers and support when the person's thoughts become extreme. This support can take a variety of forms and meet a variety of needs based on the crisis situation being experienced.

In the spaces provided, journal about some of the people on your support team.

Medical Professionals

Mental Health Professionals

Support System (friends, family, etc.)

Spiritual or Religious Person

CONTRACT

If I did not name one or more people in each of the above categories, I promise to find someone and get together with that person within the next two days.

Name _____ Date _____

Witness _____ Date _____

My Changes

Teens often become stressed and anxious about something and it causes certain life changes. These can trigger a crisis situation. It is important to take the time to explore any stressor that you are extremely anxious about.

On the lines below, write about any current life event change that is extremely stressful to you right now, and then, complete the second and third columns below.

A current stressor that is causing changes in me and my life:_____

_____

_____

My Changes	Ways This Change Could or Will Affect Me as Time Goes On	Ways I Can Reduce the Stress
Example: Changes in My Emotions	*My anxiety rises, I get jittery, hysterical, can't sleep, cry, nasty to others, etc.*	*Talk with a support person. If one person doesn't help, I will go to another.*
Changes in My Emotions		
Changes in My Behavior		
Changes in My Relationships		
Changes at My Work or Volunteer Job		
Changes in Eating		
Changes in Sleeping		
Other		

My Emergency Plan

In the case of an emergency, it would be helpful for you to create a plan that you and your support people can access if you are ill, contemplating self-harm, or suicide. The best time to work on this document is when you are doing well! Continue on another page if you need more space.

My Name _____

Address _____

Phone _____ Other Phone _____

Email Address _____

Birthdate: _____

Gender: Female _____   Male _____   Other _____

Emergency Contact: Who would you like to have notified if you are in an emergency situation?

Name	Relationship	Phone	Other Phone	Email

Medication: What are the medications you are taking, and why are you taking them.

Medication	What is it for?	OTC or RX?	Who Prescribed it?	Dosage

Service Providers: Who are your medical and mental health professionals?

Provider	Name	Phone	Address

Spiritual or Religious: List the leader(s) with whom you would like to be in contact.

Facility	Name	Phone	Address

I promise to contact the person(s) on this list if needed.

_____   _____
MY SIGNATURE   DATE

My Warning Signs

It is important to recognize and be aware of when your warning signs might put you in jeopardy of being in crisis. This will let you know that you need help – NOW!

In the circles below, write how you will know when you are experiencing your particular type of warning signs (chest feels tight, shallow breathing, feeling jittery, thoughts of harming self, etc.) of self-injury or a suicide crisis, indicating you need to ask your support people for help.

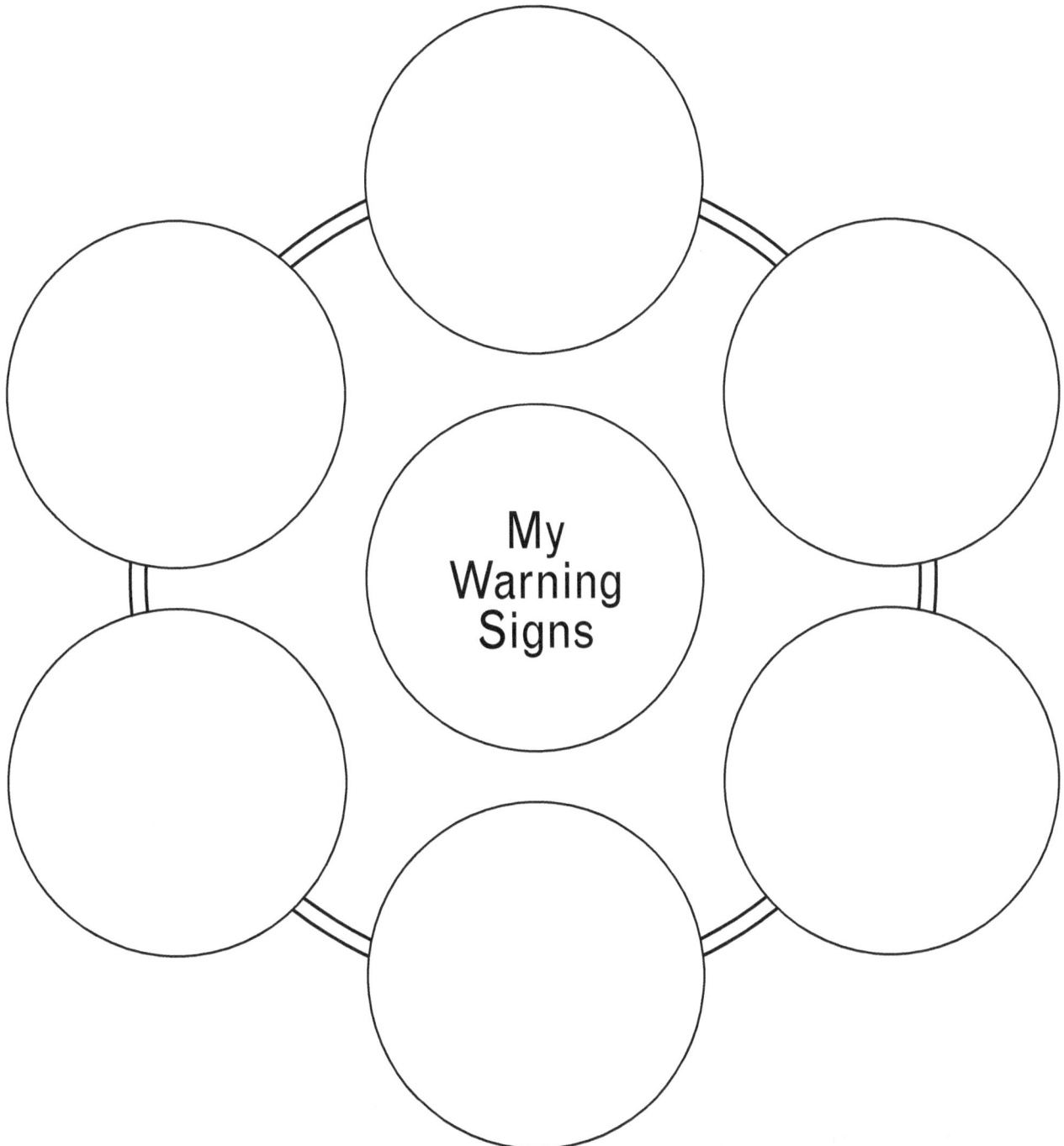

My
Warning
Signs

Remember that if you are in crisis and need immediate assistance,
call your local emergency services number (911)
or go to your closest hospital or urgent care center if your support people are not available.

What My Situation Looks Like

If you have thought about harming yourself, your situation probably has a certain look and feel to it. It may look like you are trapped in a box or look like you are sitting in a dark room all by yourself.

Imagine what your situation looks like to you, and draw, doodle, make a collage of magazine or computer cutouts, or describe it below. You may also use another sheet of paper.

Imagine what your situation would look like to you, if you could work it out and make it better.

After you are done, place a large X on the top picture and a big check mark on the lower picture. With whom can you talk to help you figure out how you can plan to work it out?

_____

_____

Support from Others

When people are having thoughts of self-harm or suicide, they often isolate themselves, which only makes their situation worse. An important factor in coping with life's challenges is having the support of others.

Even when you are not comfortable talking about your feelings, it is important to share your life's narratives. Share aspects of your story to make the emotional pain easier. Friends, family, and medical professionals in your support system can listen to you, help you process emotions, and help you make sense of what you are experiencing.

Below, list family members and/or friends who do or can provide you with support.

Family/Friends (Name Code)	The Way this Person Supports Now	What Else I Need from This Person
Example: M.S.J.	He tells me how much he loves me and how much he wants me to be well.	As soon as I start to tell him what's on my mind he gets busy and walks away. I need him to listen.

Below, list medical professionals who do or can provide you with support.

Med. Pro. (Name Code)	The Way this Person Supports Now	What Else I Need from This Person
Example: D.R.S.	He tells me to call ANY TIME that I feel the need.	I cannot get a hold of him. He sometimes calls two days later.

Using the words you wrote in the third column in both of the tables above, respectfully asking for their help, either read it to those people or write a note stating what you wrote.

Controlling Those Feelings

It is important to monitor your feelings so they do not get out of control. By identifying any early warning signs and symptoms, you can prevent a crisis from occurring. You will be able to notice the difference between your feelings during positive situations and negative situations, and you will be aware of when to take care of yourself and when to ask for help.

When you are feeling positive ...

What are you doing? _____
_____
_____

Who are you with? _____
_____
_____

Where are you? _____
_____
_____

What's going on? _____
_____
_____

When you are feeling negative ...

What are you doing? _____
_____
_____

Who are you with? _____
_____
_____

Where are you? _____
_____
_____

What's going on? _____
_____
_____

Some of the ways that you can alter these negative feelings is to call and talk with a friend, meditate, or make sure your thoughts are not fueling your feelings.

© 2019 WHOLE PERSON ASSOCIATES, 101 WEST 2ND STREET, SUITE 203, DULUTH MN 55802 • 800-247-6789 • WHOLEPERSON.COM

A Safety Agreement

By filling in the blanks on this agreement, you will agree to live the rest of your life safely and in a way that will not induce self-injury of any kind.

Complete this agreement, then sign and date it. Keep it handy so that you can see it daily.

I, _____ , agree not to harm myself in any way.
NAME

I will not try to escape the pain of my trauma by doing any of the following:

- Use any illegal substances such as _____

  _____

- Mutilate my body by _____

  _____

- Harm myself by _____

  _____

- Engage in high-risk activities such as _____

  _____

I agree to seek professional help when I feel _____

_____

_____

_____

Who I agree to see: _____

You may benefit by having a supportive person co-sign this with you.
Make a copy for each of you and for any other supportive person you wish to have one.

_____   _____
MY SIGNATURE   DATE

_____   _____
MY COSIGNER'S SIGNATURE   DATE

Let's Celebrate!

It is important to celebrate when you are tempted, but successful in remaining safe! This celebration can be done by yourself or with your support team. By celebrating your successes, you will gain the hope and momentum to keep going. Even if you do not want to tell everyone about your success in not harming yourself, you may want to tell your primary support team so that they can celebrate with you.

Members of my primary support team:

_____

_____

_____

_____

Healthy, safe ways I will celebrate with my support team:

_____

_____

_____

Healthy, safe ways I will celebrate by myself:

_____

_____

_____

Now that I have reached _____ days without harming myself, I am especially proud that:

_____

_____

_____

Great job! It is important to remember that if you relapse, you should not be angry with yourself. See it as a learning experience by asking yourself: *"What are the triggers that I encountered? What could I have done differently?"* Just because you slipped does not mean that you are starting at square one. Remember to take one day at a time and continue to move forward. There are good days ahead for you!

Find or Start a Support Group

Because many other people are experiencing exactly what you are going through, you don't have to go through your crisis by yourself. Their situations may be different, but they are in the same emotional pain that you are in.

Talking with people who understand what you are going through is one of the very best ways to cope with self-harm and/or suicidal thoughts and feelings. In support groups, you can find comfort by talking to other people who have harmed themselves, who have suicidal thoughts, or who have attempted suicide in the past.

It would be helpful to be a part of a social network of understanding people who can help you through difficult times. You can get information about support groups by contacting your local Community Service Board, therapist, or local hospital. You can search on the web support groups in your city.

It is important to have a professional lead the group.

A support group is a safety net, a place to share.

The group:
- Is a safe place to express feelings and frustrations.
- Offers confidentiality, allowing people to share similar emotions.
- Reduces feelings of isolation.
- Builds a support network that may go beyond the group setting.

A caregiver support group is a place to share and learn:
- Information.
- Coping strategies.
- Solutions to common problems.
- Techniques for dealing with family members.

Complete the following information related to a support group in your area:

A local support group in my area:_____

Time and place the group meets: _____

What I hope to receive from the group: _____

Quotes about Self-Harm

On the lines that follow, describe what each of these quotes means to you and how each applies to YOUR life.

Be strong, be fearless, be beautiful. And believe that anything is possible when you have the right people there to support you.

~ **Misty Copeland**

_____

_____

_____

_____

_____

_____

_____

Choose to focus your time, energy and conversation around people who inspire you, support you and help you to grow you into your happiest, strongest, wisest self.

~ **Karen Salmansohn**

_____

_____

_____

_____

_____

_____

_____

CHAPTER 6

Clinician and Teen Participant Resources

> The resources that follow are designed to provide you with additional information about self-injury and suicide prevention.
>
> *As the facilitator, these resources can be used by you in a variety of ways:*
>
> - You can use them to learn more about suicide, self-harm, and suicide prevention.
> - You can reproduce and distribute appropriate handouts to participants in your group and/or people supporting people in your group.
> - You can use them to supplement your sessions.

How is Self-Harm Treated?

Therapy Can Be Used to Help a Person Stop Engaging in Self-Harm

- Cognitive-behavioral therapy might be used to help an individual learn to recognize and address triggering feelings in healthier ways.

- Post-traumatic stress therapies might be helpful for self-injurers who have a history of abuse or incest.

- Group therapy might be helpful in decreasing the shame associated with self-harm, and in supporting healthy expression of emotions.

- Family therapy can help to address any history of family stress related to the behavior, and can help family members learn to communicate more directly and non-judgmentally with each other.

- In addition, hypnosis or other self-relaxation techniques are helpful in reducing the stress and tension that often precede incidents of self-injury.

- Medicines such as antidepressants or anti-anxiety medicine might be used to reduce the initial impulsive response to stress.

Causes of Self-Harm

There's no one single or simple cause that leads someone to self-harm.

In general:

- Non-suicidal self-harm is usually the result of an inability to cope in healthy ways with psychological pain.
- The person has a hard time regulating, expressing or understanding emotions. The mix of emotions that triggers self-injury is complex. For instance, there may be feelings of worthlessness, loneliness, panic, anger, guilt, rejection, self-hatred or confused sexuality.

Through self-injury, the person may be trying to ...

- Manage or reduce severe distress or anxiety and provide a sense of relief.
- Provide a distraction from painful emotions through physical pain.
- Feel a sense of control over his or her body, feelings or life situations.
- Feel something — anything — even if it's physical pain, when feeling emotionally empty.
- Express internal feelings in an external way.
- Communicate depression or distressful feelings to the outside world.
- Be punished for perceived faults.

Excerpted from
https://www.mayoclinic.org/diseases-conditions/self-injury/symptoms-causes/syc-20350950
and used with permission from Mayo Foundation for Medical Education and Research.
All Rights Reserved

Find Support

If you or someone you know is struggling, you are not alone. There are many supports, services and treatment options that may help. A change in behavior or mood may be the early warning signs of a mental health condition and should never be ignored. There are many different types of mental illness, and it isn't easy to simplify the range of challenges people face.

Here are some things to consider when reaching out:

- If it's an emergency in which you or someone you know is suicidal, you should immediately call the **National Suicide Prevention Lifeline at 1-800-273-8255,** call 911, or go to a hospital emergency room.

- If you can wait a few days, make an appointment with your primary healthcare provider or pediatrician if you think your condition is mild to moderate.

- If your symptoms are moderate to severe, make an appointment with a specialized doctor such as a psychiatrist. You may need to contact your community mental health center or primary health care provider for a referral.

- If you or your child is in school or at college, contact the school and ask about their support services.

- Seek out support groups in your community and educate yourself about your symptoms and diagnosis. Social support and knowledge can be valuable tools for coping.

> **Printed with permission of NAMI – National Alliance on Mental Illness**
> **https://www.nami.org/**
> **NAMI HelpLine: 1-800-950-NAMI (6264) or info@nami.org**

Facts about Suicide in the United States

- The annual age-adjusted suicide rate is 13.42 per 100,000 individuals.
- Men die by suicide 3.53 times more often than women.
- On average, there are 123 suicides per day.
- Firearms accounted for 51% of all suicides in 2016. The next most common methods were suffocation (including hangings) at 25.89% and poisoning at 14.90%.
- In 2016, the highest suicide rate (19.72) was among adults between 45 and 54 years of age.
- The second highest rate (18.98) occurred in those 85 years or older.
- Younger groups have had consistently lower suicide rates than middle-aged and older adults.
- In 2016, adolescents and young adults aged 15 to 24 had a suicide rate of 13.15.

Suicide Rates by Race/Ethnicity

In 2016, the highest U.S. suicide rate (15.17) was among Whites and the second highest rate (13.37) was among American Indians and Alaska Natives. Much lower and roughly similar rates were found among Asians and Pacific Islanders (6.62), and Black or African Americans (6.03). Note that the CDC records Hispanic origin separately from the primary racial or ethnic groups of White, Black, American Indian or Alaskan Native, and Asian or Pacific Islander, since individuals in all of these groups may also be Hispanic.

Suicide Attempts

No complete count is kept of suicide attempts in the U.S.; however, each year the CDC (Centers for Disease Control and Prevention) gathers data from hospitals on non-fatal injuries from self-harm as well as survey data.

In 2015, 505,507 people visited a hospital for injuries due to self-harm. This number suggests that for every reported suicide death, approximately 11.4 people visit a hospital for self-harm related injuries. However, because of the way these data are collected, we are not able to distinguish intentional suicide attempts from non-intentional self-harm behaviors.

Based on the 2016 National Survey of Drug Use and Mental Health it is estimated that 0.5 percent of the adults aged 18 or older made at least one suicide attempt. This translates to approximately 1.3 million adults. Adult females reported a suicide attempt 1.2 times as often as males. Further breakdown by gender and race are not available.

Based on the 2015 Youth Risk Behaviors Survey, 8.6 percent of youth in grades 9-12 reported that they had made at least one suicide attempt in the past 12 months. Girls attempted twice as often as boys (11.6% vs. 5.5%) and teens of Hispanic origin reported the highest rate of attempt (11.3%), especially Hispanic females (15.1%) when compared with White students (6.8%) and White females (9.8%). Approximately 2.8 percent reported making a suicide attempt that required treatment by a doctor or nurse. For those requiring treatment, rates were highest for Hispanic students with Black males (4.0%) and Hispanic males (2.9%) having higher rates than White male (0.9%) students.

When it comes to suicide and suicide attempts there are rate differences depending on demographic characteristics such as age, gender, ethnicity and race. Nonetheless, suicide occurs in all demographic groups.

**Information used with permission from the
American Foundation for Suicide Prevention
AFSP.org   1-888-333-AFSP (2377)**

How 5 Steps Can Help Someone Who Is Suicidal

1. ASK

HOW – Asking the question "Are you thinking about suicide?" communicates that you're open to speaking about suicide in a non-judgmental and supportive way. Asking in this direct, unbiased manner, can open the door for effective dialogue about their emotional pain and can allow everyone involved to see what next steps need to be taken. Other questions you can ask include, "How do you hurt?" and "How can I help?" Do not ever promise to keep their thoughts of suicide a secret.

The flip side of the "Ask" step is to "Listen." Make sure you take their answers seriously and do not ignore them, especially if they indicate they are experiencing thoughts of suicide. Listening to their reasons for being in such emotional pain, as well as listening for any potential reasons they want to continue to stay alive, are both incredibly important when they are telling you what's going on. Help them focus on their reasons for living and avoid trying to impose your reasons for them to stay alive.

WHY – Studies show that asking at-risk individuals if they are suicidal does not increase suicides or suicidal thoughts. In fact, studies suggest the opposite: findings suggest acknowledging and talking about suicide may in fact reduce rather than increase suicidal ideation.

2. KEEP THEM SAFE

HOW – First of all, it's good for everyone to be on the same page. After the "Ask" step, and you've determined suicide is indeed being talked about, it's important to find out a few things to establish immediate safety. Have they already done anything to try to kill themselves before talking with you? Does the person experiencing thoughts of suicide know how they would kill themselves? Do they have a specific, detailed plan? What's the timing for their plan? What sort of access to do they have to their planned method?

WHY – Knowing the answers to each of these questions can tell us a lot about the imminence and severity of danger the person is in. For instance, the more steps and pieces of a plan that are in place, the higher their severity of risk and their capability to enact their plan might be. Or if they have immediate access to a firearm and are very serious about attempting suicide, then extra steps (like calling the authorities or driving them to an emergency department) might be necessary. A lifeline can always act as a resource during these moments as well if you aren't entirely sure what to do next.

3. BE THERE

HOW – This could mean being physically present for someone, speaking with them on the phone when you can, or any other way that shows support for the person at risk. An important aspect of this step is to make sure you follow through with the ways in which you say you'll be able to support the person – do not commit to anything you are not willing or able to accomplish. If you are unable to be physically present with someone with thoughts of suicide, talk with them to develop some ideas for others who might be able to help as well (again, only others who are willing, able, and appropriate to be there). Listening is again very important during this step – find out what and who they believe will be the most effective sources of help.

(Continued on the next page)

How 5 Steps Can Help Someone Who Is Suicidal

3. BE THERE *(Continued)*

WHY – Being there for someone with thoughts of suicide is life-saving. Increasing someone's connectedness to others and limiting their isolation (both in the short and long-term) has shown to be a protective factor against suicide. When someone experiences this state, paired with perceived burdensomeness (arguably tied to "connectedness" through isolating behaviors and lack of a sense of purpose) and acquired capability (a lowered fear of death and habituated experiences of violence), their risk can become severely elevated.

4. HELP THEM CONNECT

HOW – Helping someone with thoughts of suicide connect with ongoing supports can help them establish a safety net for those moments they find themselves in a crisis. Additional components of a safety net might be connecting them with supports and resources in their communities. Explore some of these possible supports with them – are they currently seeing a mental health professional? Have they in the past? Is this an option for them currently? Are there other mental health resources in the community that can effectively help? One way to start helping them find ways to connect is to work with them to develop a safety plan. This can include ways for them identify if they start to experience significant, severe thoughts of suicide along with what to do in those crisis moments. A safety plan can also include a list of individuals to contact when a crisis arises.

WHY – Individuals that call a suicide prevention lifeline are significantly more likely to feel less depressed, less suicidal, less overwhelmed, and more hopeful by the end of calls handled by trained counselors. These improvements were linked to counselor interventions, including listening without judgment, exploring reasons for living and creating a network of support.

5. FOLLOW UP

HOW – After your initial contact with a person experiencing thoughts of suicide, and after you've connected them with the immediate support systems they need, make sure to follow-up with them to see how they're doing. Leave a message, send a text, or give them a call. The follow-up step is a great time to check in with them to see if there is more you are capable of helping with or if there are things you've said you would do and haven't yet had the chance to get done for the person.

WHY – This type of contact can continue to increase their feelings of connectedness and share your ongoing support. There is evidence that even a simple form of reaching out, like sending a caring postcard, can potentially reduce their risk for suicide. Studies have shown a reduction in the number of deaths by suicide when following up was involved with high risk populations after they were discharge from acute care services. Studies have also shown that brief, low cost intervention and supportive, ongoing contact may be an important part of suicide prevention.

Printed with permission from the
National Suicide Prevention Lifeline Website – 800-273-8255
https://suicidepreventionlifeline.org

Simple Things to Do to Help the Self-Harmer

It can be very difficult for a person to stop self-harming, and it may take them a long time to do so. If the person says they want to stop, discussing ways to gradually reduce the harming can sometimes be helpful. Health professionals call this harm-minimization, either reducing the severity or frequency of the self harming. The important thing here is that the person will need to find a different way of getting the emotions out.

Here are some simple things that you can do to help the self-harmer:

- Ask how they are feeling.

- Do not be judgmental.

- Do not make them feel guilty about the effect it is having on others.

- Let the person who self-harms know that you want to listen to them and hear how they are feeling when they feel ready and able to talk.

- When they do discuss it with you be compassionate and respect what the person is telling you, even though you may not understand or find it difficult to accept what they are doing.

- Do not give ultimatums such as "If you don't stop self-harming _____." This is not helpful and it won't work.

- Understand that it is a long and hard journey to stop self-harming. Be aware that someone will only stop self-harming when they feel ready and able to do so.

Printed with Permission from Befrienders Worldwide
www.befrienders.org

My Local Resources

Complete this resource information page below, make copies, and put them in several places where they are easily accessible to use if you begin to feel a need or a crisis occurring.

Name of Service Provider or Support Person	Type of Assistance	Phone Number	Address
National Suicide Prevention Hotline	Emergency Need to talk	1-800-273-8255	
911	Emergency Need to talk	911	
Nearest Hospital	Emergency Need to talk		

WholePerson

Whole Person Associates is the leading publisher of training resources for professionals who empower people to create and maintain healthy lifestyles. Our creative resources will help you work effectively with your clients in the areas of stress management, wellness promotion, mental health, and life skills.

Please visit us at our web site: **WholePerson.com**. You can check out our entire line of products, place an order, request our print catalog, and sign up for our monthly special notifications.

Whole Person Associates
800-247-6789
Books@WholePerson.com